Consumer Law
in the EEC

AUSTRALIA AND NEW ZEALAND
The Law Book Company Ltd.
Sydney : Melbourne : Perth

CANADA AND U.S.A.
The Carswell Company Ltd.
Agincourt, Ontario

INDIA
N. M. Tripathi Private Ltd.
Bombay
and
Eastern Law House Private Ltd.
Calcutta *and* Delhi
M.P.P. House
Bangalore

ISRAEL
Steimatzky's Agency Ltd.
Jerusalem : Tel Aviv : Haifa

MALAYSIA : SINGAPORE : BRUNEI
Malayan Law Journal (Pte.) Ltd.
Singapore

PAKISTAN
Pakistan Law House
Karachi

Consumer Law in the EEC

Edited by

Geoffrey Woodroffe, M.A. (Cantab.)
Solicitor, Senior Lecturer in Law
and Director of the Centre for Consumer Law Research,
Brunel University

London
Sweet & Maxwell
Centre for Consumer Law Research
1984

Published in 1984 by
Sweet & Maxwell Ltd. of
11 New Fetter Lane, London
Computerset by Promenade Graphics Limited, Cheltenham
and printed in Great Britain by
Page Bros. (Norwich) Limited

British Library Cataloguing in Publication Data
Woodroffe, G. F.
Consumer law in the EEC.
1. Consumer protection.—Law and legislation
—European Economic Community countries
I. Title
342.3'71'094 [Law]

ISBN 0-421-32640-9

All rights reserved.
No part of this publication may be
reproduced or transmitted, in any form
or by any means, electronic, mechanical, photocopying,
recording or otherwise, or stored in any retrieval
system of any nature, without the written permission
of the copyright holder and the publisher, application
for which shall be made to the publisher.

©
Geoffrey Woodroffe
1984

Preface

This book comprises nine papers delivered at a conference entitled "The Impact of European Community Law on United Kingdom Consumer Law," held in September 1983. The conference was sponsored by the Commission of the European Communities and arranged under the aegis of the Consumer Law Group which was formed in 1979 with the support of the Society of Public Teachers of Law.

The authors are all experts in the particular aspects of consumer law on which they write and more importantly on the interaction between the relevant United Kingdom law and existing or prospective Community law. As most of the authors are senior officials of the EEC Commission, the book provides a rare, if not unique, insight into the policies and philosophies underlying the EEC Consumer Protection Programme.

The book falls into four parts: (1) Introduction; (2) Advertising and Marketing; (3) Consumer Protection and Competition Law; (4) Product Liability.

Introduction. The first paper, by George Close of the Commission's Legal Service, analyses the legal basis for the EEC Consumer Protection Programme with particular reference to Articles 100 and 235 of the Treaty of Rome. This is followed by a report on the progress made so far in the Programme by Ludwig Kraemer, of the Commission's Consumer Protection Service: he considers such matters as health and safety, price control and consumer information.

Advertising and Marketing. This part of the book consists of three papers. Sidney Freedman, another senior official of the Commission's Consumer Protection Service, analyses the proposed Directive on Misleading and Unfair Advertising, now simplified and reduced in scope to omit unfair and comparative advertising in response to objections from some Member States. The need for such a Directive is questioned by Peter Thomson, Director-General of the Advertising Standards Authority, who describes the operation of the CAP—in this context meaning the Code of Advertising Practice—considers some of the criticisms of self regulation and suggests that the ASA/CAP system may work better than some commentators suggest. The third paper in this section, by Ludwig Kraemer, considers a number of marketing practices on which proposals are under discussion at Community level including premium offers, doorstep contracts and unfair contract terms.

Consumer Protection and Competition Policy. In the first of the two papers in this part Jules Stuyck, of the University of Leuven, analyses in detail the *Cassis de Dijon* decision and related case law of the European Court of Justice and reflects upon the significance for the Community and individual Member States of these cases on the free

v

movement of goods. The importance for national law of such decisions is highlighted in the paper by Patrick Deboyser, at the time of the conference the legal officer of BEUC but now an official of the Commission, who discusses the effect on redress by the individual consumer of the developments in EEC competition law.

Product Liability. The two final chapters are concerned with the increasingly important topic of product liability. A wide ranging paper by Hans Claudius Taschner, from Directorate-General III of the European Commission, surveys the national law of most European countries, both inside and outside the Community, and proceeds to give a comparative description of both the EEC draft Directive and the Council of Europe's Convention. Finally Professor Aubrey Diamond, Director of the Institute of Advanced Legal Studies, concentrates upon perhaps the most important area of product liability—the pharmaceutical industry—discussing such important aspects as the state of the art and, most topically, the voluntary system introduced by the Association of the British Pharmaceutical Industries for compensating people injured during trials of new drugs.

It can be seen that the book is not intended as a handbook of the national consumer law of each of the Member States. Nor does it attempt to analyse in depth all Community initiatives in the field. It is hoped, however, that the discussion of the important areas covered by the papers will be of interest both to those in academic life, be they students or teachers, and to those in practice, particularly in commerce and industry.

I would like to express my thanks to all the contributors and to the publishers. My particular thanks go to the officials of the Consumer Protection Service of D.G. XI (the Directorate-General for Environment, Consumer Protection and Nuclear Safety); without their support and assistance, not least of Ludwig Kraemer and Jeremiah Sheehan, the Director of the Service, the conference would not have taken place and thus this book would not have been available.

Farnham, Surrey.
June 1984
Geoffrey Woodroffe

Contents

Preface v

A. INTRODUCTION

I. The Legal Basis for the Consumer Protection Programme of the EEC and Priorities for Action

George Close 1

II. European Consumer Protection—A Progress Report

Ludwig Kraemer 25

B. ADVERTISING AND MARKETING

III. Proposed EEC Directive on Misleading and Unfair Advertising

Sidney Freedman 39

IV. Self-Regulation—Some Observations from the Advertising Standards Authority

Peter Thomson 53

V. Marketing Practices

Ludwig Kraemer 69

C. CONSUMER PROTECTION AND COMPETITION LAW

VI. Free Movement of Goods and Consumer Protection

Jules Stuyck 77

VII. Consumer Redress Under E.C. Competition Law

Patrick Deboyser 103

D. PRODUCT LIABILITY

VIII. Product Liability—Actual Legislation and Law Reform in Europe

Hans Claudius Taschner   113

IX. Product Liability and Pharmaceuticals in the United Kingdom

Aubrey L. Diamond   129

I

The Legal Basis for the Consumer Protection Programme of the EEC and Priorities for Action

George Close[1]

INTRODUCTION

It is symptomatic of the slow progress which the Consumer Protection Programme of the European Economic Community has made that there should still exist so much doubt over the preliminary question, as to whether there exists a sufficient legal basis in the Treaty establishing the EEC for the programme, and over the related question of how to justify the measures proposed and adopted in the framework of that programme in relation to the articles selected as the appropriate legal basis. For the "consumerist," anxious to make progress with substantive measures, the debate may at first sight appear a sterile one, but as this paper will seek to show, the debate is of a certain interest, because it sheds light on important aspects of the nature of the Common Market itself and also the way forward to the accomplishment of the programme.

As is well known the EEC Treaty was drafted at a time when the consumer movement was in its early stages. Its prima facie orientation is moreover that, in general, consumer interests will be sufficiently catered for by an increase in production, free movement of goods and services, the increase of competition in the market and the development of the policies expressly envisaged.[2] The result is that the Treaty does not lay down the basis for a consumer protection policy and there is a complete absence of any statement of the principles which should govern the development of such a policy. This legislative void does not necessarily mean that such a policy may not be developed. The Treaty is one of considerable flexibility and contains legal bases for action, in particular Articles 100 and 235, which offer the possibility of action in fields not expressly envisaged by the Treaty. The absence of any explicit basis for a consumer protection policy has, however, caused a considerable divergence of attitudes to

---

[1] Principal Legal Adviser, Commission of the European Communities. The views expressed in this paper, are those of the author and are not to be attributed to the Commission of the European Communities.
[2] See Bourgoignie, "Vers un droit européen de consommation? Possibilités et limites." *Revue trimestrielle de droit européenne*, No 1, January-March 1982, p.17.

exist as to whether there exists a sufficiently broad legal basis for such a policy and, if so, as regards its extent.

For the purposes of presentation it is possible to classify the attitudes to the question of the legal basis for consumer protection measures into three main groups. First, there is the extremely restrictive approach, which denies the existence of a sufficient legal basis for many kinds of consumer protection measures or only admits the possibility that such measures might be adopted by the EEC in extremely restricted circumstances. Secondly, at the other extreme, there is a liberal approach, which in general sees no particular problem in finding a legal basis for such measures. Thirdly, there is an intermediate position. In Part I of this paper each approach will be discussed in turn and there will be a brief survey of the actual evolution of attitudes. Part II will then consider whether the debate has any lessons for the orientations which the Consumer Protection Policy should take.

PART I

The restrictive approach

As regards the first approach it must be noted that it is impossible for the opponents of an EEC consumer protection programme to deny that national measures laying down product standards for the protection of the health of the consumer fall within the ambit of action based on Article 100.[3] Such measures have a direct impact on the functioning of the Common Market because they hinder the free circulation of goods. Not all consumer protection measures are, however, of this nature. If they are to be justified in accordance with the requirements of Article 100, an argument has to be developed that the national measures in question directly affect the establishment or functioning of the Common Market in some way. In practice the argument that the national measures to be harmonised create unequal conditions of competition for the enterprises which operate in the relevant sector of the market is the most often employed for this purpose.

The Danish report to the 1982 FIDE Congress held at Dublin on Consumer Protection and the Common Market[4] correctly points out that, if the functioning of the Common Market is regarded as being affected by unequal conditions of competition, the scope of Article 100 is very broad indeed, because much, if not most, of national legislation affects the conditions of competition of enterprises in some way. Harmonisation of such legislation will therefore make the conditions of competition more equal. The Danish report, moreover,

---

[3] Art. 100 provides: "The Council shall, acting unanimously on a proposal from the Commission, issue directives for the approximation of such provisions laid down by law, regulation or administrative action in Member States as directly affect the establishment or functioning of the Common Market."
[4] By Jurgen Hammer Hansen and Claus Gulmann.

draws attention to the Messina report[5] and quotes the passage which examines whether it is necessary to harmonise all the principal elements which go to make up the cost price before a valid competition between enterprises in the Common Market can be established. The report concludes to the contrary having regard to the fact that differences in such matters as social security charges are normally compensated by generally binding conditions and in particular exchange rates. The Messina Report concludes that only a limited action on the basis of Article 100 is needed, this being an action to correct or eliminate specific distortions which favour or disfavour certain sectors of activity.

The Danish report concludes therefore that:

"Article 100 cannot and should not be interpreted as giving authority to harmonise each time it is arguable that a harmonisation may further equal conditions for enterprises. A limitation on the use of Article 100 is certainly also indicated by the express condition contained in Article 100 that the functioning of the Common Market must be directly affected."

And further:

"The Danish Government is said not to feel convinced that all the actions, which according to the consumer protection programme have to be taken at the Community level, have sufficient legal basis in the treaty."

It should be noted in passing here that even if this argument for a restrictive interpretation of Article 100 were to be accepted, certain consumer protection measures would be legally justified on the basis that:

(i) their justification was not based on distortion of competition (*e.g.* the justification might be that the relevant national measures concerned directly affected the functioning of the Common Market because they hindered the free circulation of goods or services);
(ii) the national measures concerned created specific distortions;
(iii) a legal basis for the measure other than Article 100 could be found, *e.g.* it might be within one of the other policies of the Treaty (such as agriculture, transport or the provision of services) or a legal basis might be found in the shape of Article 235.[6]

---

[5] Rapport des Chefs de Délégation aux ministres des affaires étrangères (Comité intergouvernemental crée par la Conférence de Messine), Bruxelles April 21, 1980.
[6] Art. 235 provides: "If action by the Community should prove necessary to attain in the course of the operation of the Common Market one of the objectives of the Community and this Treaty has not provided the necessary powers, the Council shall, acting unanimously on a proposal from the Commission and after consulting the Assembly, take appropriate measures."

The liberal approach

Although the tenants of the liberal approach recognise the absence in the EEC Treaty of any express general policy for the protection of consumers,[7] the lack of any powers expressly envisaging Community action for this purpose does not in their view prevent such a policy being developed.

If the tenants of the liberal approach share the same conclusion, they do not necessarily arrive there by means of the same arguments. It is possible to distinguish three different tendencies amongst them (although it must be stressed that these tendencies may have much in common).

The first tendency centres on the objectives of the Treaty and the tasks conferred on the Community by Article 2 of the EEC Treaty. In the latter the following tasks are laid down: a harmonious development of economic activities; a continuous and balanced expansion; an increase in stability; an accelerated raising of the standard of living; closer relations between Member States.

It is not difficult to see, in certain of these tasks at least, the germ of consumer protection measures, particularly when read in the light of the preamble to the EEC Treaty, which refers *inter alia* to the economic and social progress of their countries by common action to eliminate the barriers which divide Europe and the constant improvement of living and working conditions of their peoples.

Having regard to the political green light given to the Consumer Protection Programme by the Paris meeting in 1972 of the Heads of State and Governments, with an approving nod in favour of Article 235 as a possible legal basis,[8] it seemed (at the time at least) that this analysis was sufficient. The early proposals of the Commission and the preamble to the Preliminary Programme of the European Community for a consumer protection programme and information policy strongly reflect this approach.[9]

A second tendency is to regard the problem of the legal basis, given the broad objectives of the EEC Treaty, as more of a political problem than a legal one. Given the somewhat elastic quality of Community Law this view is not implausible, even if to a lawyer it may appear somewhat unsatisfactory. A good example of this

---

[7] Reference is made to consumers in several Articles of the Treaty, *i.e.* 39, 79, 85 and 86.

[8] Relevant extracts from the Declaration are as follows: " . . . Whereas the tasks of the Community are increasing and new responsibilities are conferred on it . . . .
Economic expansion, which is not an end in itself, must have as a priority the reduction in the differences in conditions of life. It must be pursued with the participation of all the social partners. It must show itself by an improvement in both the quality and the standard of living.
This programme (*i.e.* the action programme) must aim at reinforcing and co-ordinating actions in favour of the protection of consumers . . . .
It is appropriate to use as much as possible all the provisions of the Treaty, including Article 235 of the EEC Treaty."

[9] See Annex, points 1 and 2.

approach is to be found in the EEC Report on Consumer Protection and the Common Market by Jeremiah P. Sheehan.[10] The tenants of this approach, however, also deploy some arguments in order to overcome resistance to their proposals, which may be analysed from a legal viewpoint. Two principal arguments are so used (apart from the general need to protect consumers), these being based first on the objectives of the EEC Treaty and secondly on the essentially distorting effect on the conditions of competition of national consumer protection measures. The argument is extremely far reaching. Thus in the above-mentioned report it is stated that "by virtue of the existence of national regulations in the field of consumer protection, whatever may be the form of the protection that they are intended to provide, then Community competence is necessarily involved once an inequality of provision occurs between Member States" (pp. 11–14).

The tendency described above finds an echo in the preambles of the early measures of consumer protection proposed by the Commission.[11]

The third tendency is a result of the need to deepen the initial analysis made in the face of opposition and criticism to the proposals of the Commission. It rests upon an analysis of the nature of a market economy and the important role which the consumer plays in it. Once this is established recourse to the general powers in Articles 100 and 235 (as appropriate) as a legal basis for consumer protection measures follows without very much intellectual difficulty.[12]

Very briefly the argument is as follows. The Common Market is a market economy. For a market to function, goods[13] must be produced and sold. If this aspect of the market has been the main preoccupation until relatively recently of the economic measures adopted under the Treaty, it is nonetheless incontestable that the production/sale side of the market only represents one aspect of it. A market economy does not function without the correlative activities of purchase/consumption. It would be a great mistake to conceive the purchase/consumption function as a purely passive activity, that is to say that the average citizen merely purchases and consumes what is produced and offered for sale without producing any feedback on what he is offered. The importance of the role of the consumer is particularly strong in a liberal economy where the principle of competition has been given the role of the engine of evolution in the market, as is the case with the Common Market. The choices of

---

[10] For example, at p. 11.6 (*op. cit.*): "I see little to dispute the conclusion that in the present situation, the problems of expanding the Community's statute book in the field of consumer protection and information are political and economic, not legislative."
[11] See points 4 and 5 in the Annex.
[12] See G.L. Close, "Harmonisation of Laws : Use or Abuse of the Powers under the EEC Treaty?" (1978) 3 E.L. Rev. 461.
[13] Goods in this context also include services.

the consumers and the conditions in which they are exercised become therefore an important regulatory feature of the market.[14] The need for a consumer policy is all the greater in the enlarged market created by the EEC Treaty, where the disequilibrium between producers/distributors and producers/consumers may be further aggravated.[15]

The tenants of the liberal approach not only would advocate recourse to Article 100 (in particular where national measures of consumer protection produce distortions of competition—here sharply differing from the tenants of the restrictive approach) but also rely on the potentialities of Article 235.[16] If there are certain limitations which prevent Article 100 being retained as a legal basis in particular cases (*e.g.* complete absence of national measures to be harmonised, uncertainty as to whether the direct effect on the functioning of the Common Market can be established,[17] harmonisation not being an aim of the measure, unsuitability of a directive as the legal form of Community action, etc.), recourse can usually be had to Article 235.[18]

Of course, Article 235 is not a means whereby the Treaty can be extended beyond its proper scope and Article 235 itself contains limitations, particularly that the action based on the article must be necessary to attain one of the objectives of the Community and this action must be linked to the operation of the Common Market. On the analysis made above, however, these conditions are not usually difficult to fulfil.

As regards the question whether a particular proposal fulfils the requirements of Article 235, the answer will of course depend on the substantive content of the proposal, but it is difficult to conceive a general measure of consumer protection which does not have a link between it and the functioning of the Common Market because of the role which consumers play in the market economy. Moreover the objectives of the measure will usually correspond to those set out in the Treaty, for example the raising of the standard of living or harmonious economic development, because it would be a rare consumer protection measure which was not designed to have these effects.

---

[14] In the same sense see "Mölichkeiten und Grenzen der Verbraucherpolitik im Gemeinsamen Markt," *Europarecht*, No. 3 July-September 1981, p. 240; and para. 47 of the second programme of the EEC for a consumer protection and information policy, which reads " . . . consumption should no longer be regarded merely as a balancing variable of economic development." The logical consequences of this are, however, only developed as regards consumer consultation.
[15] See Bourgoignie (*op. cit.*), p. 17.
[16] This, of course, corresponds to the original statement made on consumer protection policy by the Heads of State in October 1972 in Paris.
[17] If the economic role of the consumer in the market is accepted, the criterion of direct effect ceases to present a major difficulty.
[18] See points 9 and 10 of the Annex.

The intermediate position

The intermediate position is based on an ad hoc approach to the particular measure in question. A justification is developed for the measure with particular reference to the article of the Treaty being retained as the legal basis. Reference may still be made to the general objectives of the Treaty, to the general need to protect consumers and to political expressions in favour of the measure such as the Preliminary Programme, but nevertheless the core of the preamble of the measure concerned will be devoted to a detailed justification that the requirements of the article chosen as the legal basis are met on economic and practical grounds without making reference to the role of the consumer in the market. This tendency commenced with the Commission's proposal on misleading and unfair advertising[19] and has continued with the later proposals, although it is notably more relaxed in the case of the Council measures adopted on the basis of Article 235.

Some preliminary conclusions

Before proceeding further it is useful at this stage to draw some provisional conclusions from the evolution of the argument so far. As we have seen the Commission, and indeed the Member States, embarked on a consumer protection policy on the basis of a liberal interpretation of the possibilities of Article 235. In the face of hardening resistance to its proposals the tendency of the Commission has been (despite some tendency to discuss the problem as being political rather than legal), not unnaturally, to concentrate on the justification of particular measures by relating their content specifically to the requirements of the legal bases chosen, rather than developing any general theory of the role of the consumer in the market. In so doing heavy reliance has been placed on the distortion of the effects of competition by disparate national consumer measures, although this is not the only such justification used. In view of the criticism which this tendency has attracted it becomes now appropriate to analyse further the arguments in the Danish report to the 1982 FIDE Congress, with reference in particular to the Messina Report, which seems to be one of the best developed arguments against the use of this type of justification.

The argument in the Messina Report

First, it is to be noticed that the Messina Report addresses itself to the problem of whether a valid competition can be established between enterprises before all the elements resulting from the legislative and reglementary functions of the Member States, which make up the cost price, are harmonised. The Report points out that the exchange rate compensates for certain differences in the con-

---

[19] See point 6 of the Annex.

ditions of competition, but recognises that harmonisation will be necessary where specific distortions are created which favour or disfavour certain sectors of activity.

It is very doubtful, however, whether the Messina Report should be interpreted as imposing a limitation on the possibilities of harmonisation under Article 100. The point to which it was addressing itself was whether a valid competition between enterprises could be established in the early stages of the establishment of the Common Market without very extensive harmonisation. The fact that this was possible does not rule out subsequent measures of harmonisation so as to eliminate other distortions, which nevertheless were not of such a nature as to invalidate the original inauguration of the Common Market.[20]

Further it is to be noted that with the introduction of the European Monetary System, which attempts to stabilise the currencies of the Member States which participate in relation to each other, one of the principal mechanisms on which the Messina Report relied to compensate for distortions of competition has become less effective. It must follow therefore that a greater emphasis must be put on harmonisation.

Thirdly, if flexibility in exchange rates produces a certain equilibrium between economies generally, it would not be expected that this mechanism would produce an exact correspondence of advantages and disadvantages as between all particular sectors of activity in different economies. Article 100 therefore retains its full importance for this purpose.

Finally the important differences between Articles 100 and 101 of the Treaty are to be noticed. It would seem that Article 101 has been designed to cover the case of a specific distortion of the conditions of competition, but that no such limitation appears in Article 100. To restrict the latter article in this fashion would be to go against the system of the Treaty.

---

[20] Section 2 of Chapter 2 of the Messina Report indicates more clearly the progressive nature of harmonisation, which appears from the following passages:
"Les clauses de sauvegarde pallient les effets dommageables des distorsions. Toutefois de simples compensations temporaires, par exemple une aide spéciale ou une protection particulière aux industries qui se révèlent désavantagées, n'apparaissent pas comme une solution valable à défaut d'un mécanisme qui aboutisse à les rendre inutiles. Dans certains cas, il pourra apparaître que la meilleure manière de faire disparaître la distorsion soit de rapprocher dans les différents pays des dispositions légales dont la disparité provoque cette distorsion même."
" ... Même sans être une condition absolue du fonctionnement du marché commun, une unification du système d'impôts, par exemple, permettant d'écarter les exonérations et compensations à l'intérieur du marché commun et par conséquent les contrôles douaniers, ou aussi bien une unification des systèmes de sécurité sociale, éliminerait de sérieux obstacles à la circulation des marchandises et des personnes."
" ... En ce qui concerne les conditions de travail, on concevrait difficilement le maintien de régimes sensiblement différents à l'intérieur d'un marché commun."

It would follow from the above considerations that arguments drawn from the Messina Report are a very doubtful basis for justifying the restrictive approach. It may be concluded therefore that, so far at least, very little intellectual foundation for the restrictive approach has been demonstrated. It would, however, be premature to conclude that the liberal approach has gained the day. The hesitations of Member States will continue to be such that for political reasons at least the intermediate approach will continue to be appropriate, even if every attempt should be made to understand the role of the consumer as a market mechanism.

PART II

Law and policy

It is at this point that it becomes important to widen the debate, because behind the arguments about a legal foundation for the Community's consumer protection programme are more fundamental reservations of a political nature. Undoubtedly, the Member States are reluctant to see an important expansion of the competence of the Community in areas where the justification for Community activity is not expressly laid down by the Treaty. Added to this are considerations based on the opportuneness of such action at a time of economic recession, the sensitivity of Member States to action by the Community in areas which affect well established and traditional law (*e.g.* contract and negligence law) and perhaps a certain jealousy over Community activity in an area which has such a direct impact on the public.

The best way out of this impasse is to establish in a more vigorous and compelling way the justification and the opportuneness of Community activity. In this sense legal and political considerations largely coincide.

Opportuneness of Community action for consumer protection

The boldest and perhaps the best way would be to try to convince Member States of the significance of the role of the consumer in the market. Given however the intermediate approach adopted by the Commission, it is possible also to develop its inherent logic. In the context of the present analysis there are two important general considerations in operation with respect to the opportuneness of Community action for consumer protection. The first is the appropriateness of any action at all, irrespective of by whom or how it is taken. Thus certain Member States may take the view that priority should be given to increasing production or competition and that consumer interests can look after themselves, whereas others may, being for the time-being satisfied on this score, be prepared to move on to a subsequent phase. The second principal consideration is the degree of attachment which is perceived of the proposed measure to the Common Market, ranging from on the one hand the attitude that this is a matter which should be dealt with by Brussels to, on the other hand, the attitude that this is a matter for state or local action. These considerations can be plotted as two axes.[21]

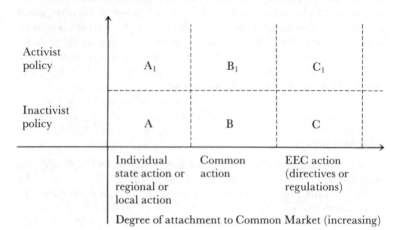

Figure 1

Zones A, B and C (on the inactivism-activism axis) represent areas where Member States see no or little need for action to protect consumers. Where they can be persuaded that some minimal action nevertheless needs to be taken, the choice has to be made whether this should be at national level, whether it should be taken by common action of the Member States or whether it should be taken at Community level (these zones being situated on the other axis representing the degree of attachment to the Common Market). Thus Member States may be prepared to adopt some minimal action, *e.g.* in the form of a Council Resolution or Recommendation (zone C), in the form of a common approach to a non-binding declaration in an international organisation (zone B) or to some low profile measures adopted at national or even local level (zone A).

A corresponding schema exists where there is a general consensus that action is required (see zones situated further away from zero on the inactivist-activist axis). In this case perceptions may differ as to whether action is required at Community level (zone C_1), *e.g.* by means of a directive, in the form of common action (zone B_1), *e.g.* by means of international agreement or the adoption of a model law, or at purely national, regional or local level (zone A_1).

In practice the situation is usually more complicated, with Member States holding different perceptions with respect to where the problem should be situated with respect to both axes. The position of the same Member State may also vary depending on the particu-

---

[21] Although the treatment is rather different, a debt is acknowledged to Professor Trubeck of the University of Wisconsin for this presentation.

lar consumer protection problem concerned, although certain general attitudes in capitals may enable the approach of particular Member States to be predictable irrespective of the problem concerned. And of course perceptions of Member States do change—it is now generally acknowledged that the harmonisation of product standards is Community business (zones C, C_1), even if there may be an argument as to whether action is or is not necessary. Finally it is to be noted that even if Member States can be persuaded to perceive the problem in the same way (*i.e.* occupy the same zone), there may still exist considerable argument as to the precise action appropriate. If, for example, Member States are persuaded that action is necessary and that it should take the form of common action (zone B_1), there may still be considerable scope for discussion whether the action should take the form of *e.g.*: a convention to be negotiated between Member States (and possibly third countries); a co-ordinated position based on a Community discipline towards negotiations in an international framework; the participation in such negotiations subject to such a discipline; the establishment of a model law, code of conduct, universally agreed standards for voluntary incorporation, etc.

It is also noteworthy that the interests of the consumerists do not necessarily coincide with the zones furthest from zero on the horizontal axis, that is that they are not necessarily better served by the matter being generally perceived as belonging to zone C rather than to zone A. Zone C may represent a particularly frustrating situation, for a proposal may be blocked at EEC level and efforts to push the matter forward on the national level may well be met by the argument that nothing should be done because it is being treated at an EEC level.

Before progress can be made in the present intellectual context in which the Community consumer protection policy is perceived some general agreement needs to be reached as to where particular problems should be situated in the schema discussed above. Of course political considerations, questions of opportunity and chance factors will always play a role in influencing the decision on this allocation, particularly whether something needs to be done (activism versus inactivism), but nevertheless the time has come for an attempt to be made to disengage some more general criteria whereby this allocation can be made.

Degree of attachment to the Common Market

As has been pointed out earlier, although there is a basic distinction to be made between law and policy, there is a certain similarity between the problem of deciding whether there is a proper legal basis (in the context of the intermediate approach) and the problem of whether action should be taken at Community level, in that both questions depend on a firm link being made with the Common Market. If the criteria are more formal for the legal basis ("directly affect the Common Market" (Article 100) or "action ... necessary to attain, in the course of the operation of the Common Market, one of the objectives of the Community" (Article 235)), nevertheless a certain measure of political judgment seems inescapable in their application—a judgment which is also of importance in deciding both priorities and whether the action should take place.

Although the concept of the "Common Market" varies somewhat in the Treaty,[22] the sense in which it is used in Articles 100 and 235 seems to be the basic principles and policies laid down by the Treaties establishing the Community, that is to say: the customs union; the free circulation of goods, persons, services and capital; the common policies in the fields of agriculture, transport and external commerce; the establishment of an undistorted system of competition; social policy and such other activities as are envisaged by the Treaty.

In addition it should be borne in mind that the Common Market is not a static concept in the sense that there is a precise blue print for it, with the result that at some point it will be possible to claim that the establishment of the Common Market has been completed. It has the more nebulous quality of organic growth—it being impossible to predict exactly what will be its final shape and what "space" it will finally occupy. If however the shape and location of the periphery remains uncertain, the core is relatively well determined and becomes increasingly more so with the legislative activity of the Council and the development of the case law of the Court of Justice.

Having regard to the foregoing it becomes possible to construct the following schema:

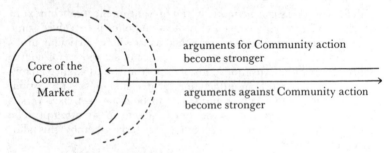

Figure 2

As will be seen as one moves towards the core, so the link with the Common Market grows stronger, with the result that the arguments for Community action become more compelling and conversely as one moves away from the core the arguments become weaker. The reason why I trouble the reader with this statement of the obvious is

---

[22] See "Harmonisation of Laws: Use or Abuse of Powers," (1978) 3 E.L. Rev. 473–476.

that the schema seems to offer the possibility of being given some operational utility. In particular it is interesting to examine whether the movement to or from the core is an undifferentiated or evenly graduated path offering little guidance as to the degree of separation from the core or whether there are indeed "land marks" on the way.

The Community spectrum

In fact far from being an undifferentiated path the passage to or from the core has more the appearance of a spectrum.

Starting from the core we encounter the following:

(1) The first compartment is that where there occurs what has come to be called "negative harmonisation."[23] This is where national measures, ostensibly adopted to protect consumers, are incompatible with the Treaty, *e.g.* with Article 30, not being saved by virtue of Article 36 or the *Cassis de Dijon* principle. It would not generally speaking be appropriate to make a proposal to harmonise incompatible measures on the basis of Article 100. The appropriate action here, if the Member State will not withdraw such measures, is for the Commission to take proceedings on the basis of Article 169. We are so well within the core here that legislative action is not necessary or even appropriate. The withdrawal of the national measures depends not on the agreement of the Member States but should have a certain inevitability. Even apart from the action of the Commission, the question may well be raised before the Court in Article 177 proceedings.

(2) Between the first compartment and the third (which is the traditional area of harmonisation of product standards, where clearly it is necessary to harmonise to enable the product to circulate without hindrance in the Common Market) there lies a grey area. It is a grey area because it may not always be easy to ascertain whether the national measures are contrary to the Treaty and the relevant case law of the Court of Justice. It would certainly be possible to refer the question to the Court, subject to material considerations as to the amount of work this would generate, but even the Court may have difficulty in determining the issue.[24] This therefore is an obscure area on the fringe of the inner core where a rather difficult decision will have to be taken as to how to proceed, *i.e.* via Article 169 (infringement proceedings) or on the basis of Article 100 (Community legislation). It may be, however, that in certain cases this would be an exceptionally interesting area in which to legislate, *e.g.* to pre-empt a judicial solution or to enable measures to be adopted

---

[23] Ole Lando, "Consumer Protection and the Common Market General Report" *FIDE Dublin* 1982, p. 1.9.

[24] For examples of cases where the issues were not clear see Case 249/81 *"Buy Irish" Commission* v. *Ireland* (not yet reported) and Case 75/81 *Blesgen* v. *Belgium* [1982] 3 E.C.R. 1211. More generally many laws which prescribe quality standards lie in this area.

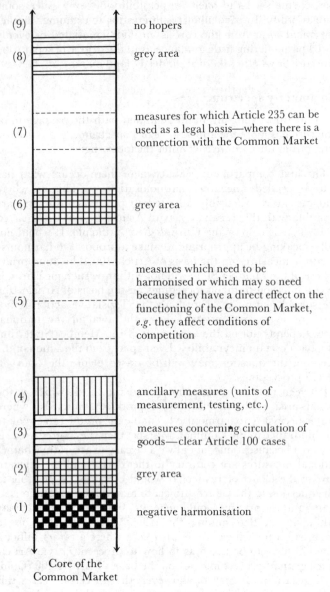

Figure 3

at Community level which might possibly go somewhat beyond what individual Member States could do.

(3) Compartment (3) is still well in contact with the inner core. There is little argument that Article 100 serves as the basis of measures designed to harmonise product standards so as to enable them to circulate freely in the Common Market. There may be dif-

ferences of opinion about priorities here, but none about the direct consequences on the functioning of the Common Market of this sort of measure. This area is principally concerned with the harmonisation of measures left to Member States under Article 36 and the *Cassis de Dijon* principle. In this area also the case law of the Court of Justice has stimulated the need for harmonisation. Member States now have to check whether imports from other Member States meet standards equivalent to their own. If so, they will have to be admitted. This may be a difficult technical and administrative exercise. A harmonisation of legislation by means of a directive based on Article 100 may well prove simpler and in consequence be welcomed by Member States.[25]

(4) In compartment (4) may be situated an ancillary group of measures, which are linked to the previous group and are designed to make the latter function. They may concern common standards of testing, most measurements, unit pricing, labelling, etc.

(5) Compartment (5) takes us into a more controversial area, where the justification for the use of Article 100 is based on an argument that the national measures concerned directly affect the functioning of the Common Market, *e.g.* conditions of competition or circulation of goods. Already there are more doubts about both the opportuneness of the measures and their legal justification, despite the case law of the Court of Justice.[26] The case for legislating on a Community level has to be carefully constructed on the basis of legal, economic and political justifications. Even within the compartment there are important gradations, because, *e.g.* for some groups of measures it may be relatively easier to demonstrate the need to legislate because of striking cases of existing distortions.

(6) There is no very clear dividing line between the measures which may be adopted on the basis of Article 100 and those which may be adopted on the basis of Article 235. There is therefore a further grey area where a difficult choice has to be made between the two Articles—a choice which may be fudged by basing the measure on both or simply having recourse to Article 235[27] as being a legal basis offering wider possibilities.

(7) In this compartment, although the link with the functioning of the Common Market still exists, it has become more attenuated, with a corresponding increase in doubts on the part of the Member States as to the opportuneness of action by the Community and indeed as to whether a legal basis exists. Again however there are

[25] In the same sense see Peter Oliver, "Measures of Equivalent Effect· A Reappraisal," (1982) 19 C.M.L. Rev. 237.
[26] In the related field of environmental protection, the Court stated, in Cases 91 and 92/79 [1980] E.C.R. 1099 and 1115, that "Directives on the environment may be based on Article 100 of the Treaty since provisions which are made necessary by the environment and health may be a burden on the undertakings to which they apply and if there is no harmonisation of national provisions on the matter competition may be distorted."
[27] See item 9 in the Annex.

certain differentiations one can make, where legal, economic or technical reasons exist to justify particular measures.[28] Particularly important is the case where national measures have pronounced cross-frontier effects, where the desirability of taking action at Community level may be more easy to justify, e.g. television advertising and credit measures. Consumer protection measures which are not concerned principally with the circulation of goods, e.g. standard contract clauses, access to justice, group actions by consumers etc., fall into this category on the basis of the intermediate approach.

(8) The limits of Article 235 are ill-defined, and therefore compartment (7) is followed by a further grey area which merges into the following where no legal basis for action exists.

(9) The final compartment is where no legal basis exists and the distance from the core is becoming considerable. Any proposal situated in this area has been labelled as a "no hoper."

To a certain extent the reluctance of Member States to envisage binding Community measures in the compartments lying further from the core is compensated by an increasing readiness to envisage soft law solutions in this area. Thus we get the following schema:

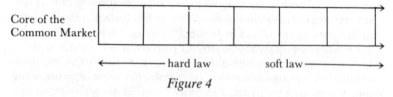

Figure 4

Soft law[29] comprises such techniques as (diminishing in "hardness") model laws for voluntary incorporation, codes of conduct, voluntary agreements with branches of industry, recommendations, resolutions and declarations, pilot projects, grants for research, etc.

Finally it should be noted that, as has been pointed out, the Common Market is not static. The core is in evolution and the perception of the Member States of the degree of connection with the core (and indeed the proper legal analysis of this question) will vary with this evolution.

Conclusions

As was shown in Part I there is little legal justification for a highly restrictive approach to a Community Consumer Protection Policy. As yet the Commission has not sought, in a convincing and systematic way, to persuade the Member States that such a policy is justified

---

[28] Thus the freedom of circulation of goods in the Common Market requires a Community framework for the efficient and speedy notification of cases where products prove to be dangerous.

[29] Reference is made in several places in the second programme of the EEC for a consumer protection and information policy to "soft" law solutions, e.g. voluntary agreements for improving services with the sector concerned.

on general economic grounds, by reference to the role which the consumer plays in the market. On the contrary it has moved towards the "intermediate" approach, according to which proposals are justified in a detailed way by reference to the legal basis chosen for them. The preambles thus attempt to show that the requirements of the Article are met by the substantive content of the proposals on grounds other than to do with the role of the consumer in the market. Given the hesitations of Member States to accept consumer protection proposals on political, economic and legal grounds this is understandable, even if finally the task of the Commission would probably be made easier by an acceptance of the role of the consumer in the market.

When presenting a proposal the Commission must demonstrate both the opportuneness of the action proposed and also the opportuneness of action at a Community level. Rather careful attention should be given to alternatives to action at this level before the latter is proposed in view of both the resistance of Member States and the blocking effect which proposals may have.

In demonstrating the need for action at Community level what is essentially involved in the intermediate approach is to show the connection with the functioning of the Common Market. Where this is demonstrated objections based on legal grounds should also be overcome.

In demonstrating the degree of connection with the Common Market different categories of measures may be distinguished, which fall into different compartments, even if there is some blurring of the edges. Some are of particular interest to the Community legislators and to the Member States (*e.g.* quality legislation—compartment 2 of the Figure on p.14), where it would seem that priority attention deserves to be given.[30] Even, however, where the degree of connection becomes more exiguous there may be a particular interest in a Community measure because of particular circumstances (*e.g.* a measure based on Article 235 on the exchange of information on defective products). The possibility of "soft law" solutions should also not be overlooked in these circumstances.

The consequences of the intermediate approach are clearly demonstrated in connection with such "real" consumer measures as standard contract terms, access for consumers to justice and group actions, which become relegated to a compartment which is situated rather far from the core of the Common Market. It is probable that, unless Member States can be persuaded to accept a new approach based on the role of the consumer in the Common Market, such proposals will be met with the greatest resistance, unless they take the form of "soft law."

---

[30] It would seem from para. 3 of the second programme that a consensus on this point could be reached, even if the Member States arrive at this conclusion via a different route, this being value for money in a difficult economic climate.

ANNEX

I. DESCRIPTION OF MEASURES AND PROPOSALS

1. Commission Decision of September 25, 1973 relating to the setting up of a Consumers' Consultative Committee (73/306/EEC)[31]

This measure is rather special as it is a decision of the Commission taken under its general powers (Article 155), but of an internal nature (*Beschluss*). It does not therefore contain a specific legal basis and is not addressed to third parties. Because of the fact that the Commission was able to take the decision itself, the justification was not subject to the approval of the Council.

The preamble recalls four of the tasks of the Community set out in Article 2 of the Treaty (constant improvement of the standard of living, harmonious development of the economies, continuous and balanced expansion and closer relations between Member States), refers to the political green light given to the consumer protection programme by the Heads of State and Governments at their conference in October 1972 in Paris and asserts that a close and continuous contact with consumer organisations at Community level can contribute to the achievement of these aims.

In view of the circumstances of the adoption of the Decision and its uncontentious content (the setting up of a consultative committee) the justification did not require to be very detailed or rigorous.

2. Council Resolution of April 14, 1975 on a preliminary programme of the European Community for a consumer protection and information policy[32]

Being a resolution, this measure does not refer to any specific article of the EEC Treaty as its legal basis. Like the previous Commission decision, the preamble makes reference to the aims in Article 2 of the EEC Treaty and to the Paris meeting, but omits to mention the aim of closer relations between Member States. It also asserts, in conformity with the communiqué of the Paris meeting, that improvement of the quality of life is one of the tasks of the Community and as such implies protecting the health, safety and economic interests of the consumer.

It was not necessary to establish a specific linkage with a particular article of the Treaty, because of the political nature of the measure.

---

[31] O.J. 1973 L283/18.
[32] O.J. 1975 C92/1.

3. Proposed Directive on liability for defective products[33]

This proposal is based on Article 100. By way of justification the following arguments are used: distortions of competition are caused by reason of the various regimes of liability in force in Member States and the resultant differences in costs to producers; differences n legal regimes can influence where goods are sold, thus influencing the free circulation of goods.

4. Proposed Directive on contracts negotiated away from business premises[34]

This proposal is based on Article 100. The justification recites that the negotiation of "doorstep" contracts is subject to the legislation of Member States, that a disparity between these legislations can have a direct effect on the functioning of the Common Market and that therefore it is appropriate to proceed to a harmonisation of the national measures. Other paragraphs recall the political orientation in favour of such a measure in the Council Resolution and refer to the need to protect consumers by appropriate measures against abusive commercial practices in the field of doorstep contracts.

This reasoning, like that of the previous proposal, is thus very wide. In particular there is no detailed reasoning to establish that the disparity of legislation in the field of doorstep selling has a direct effect on the functioning of the Common Market. This is asserted as if it is self-evident.

5. Proposed Council Directive on the protection of participants in home study courses[35]

This proposal, which is now withdrawn, was based on Article 100. The justification follows the same pattern as the previous proposal.

6. Proposed Directive relating to the approximation of laws, regulations and administrative provisions of the Member States concerning misleading and unfair advertising[36]

This proposal is made on the basis of Article 100. It recites that the national laws in force in Member States differ widely and that, since advertising reaches to a large extent beyond the frontiers of individual Member States, it has a direct effect on the establishment and the functioning of the Common Market. It also notes that unfair and misleading advertising is likely to: restrict the establishment of a system to ensure that competition is not distorted within the Common Market; lead to inadequate levels of consumer protection; prevent the execution of advertising campaigns beyond national boundaries; and consequently affect the free circulation of goods and the provision of services.

[33] O.J. 1976 C241/9.
[34] O.J. 1977 C22/6.
[35] O.J. 1977 C208/12.
[36] O.J. 1978 C70/4.

Other paragraphs in the preamble mention: the favourable reference to such a proposal in the preliminary programme; the public interest in the harmonisation of the national laws concerned; the benefits to consumer and competitor of comparative advertising.

This proposal therefore marks something of a departure from previous proposals, as it develops rather more than had been done previously arguments in support of the proposition that the disparity of the national legislation in the field concerned has a direct effect on the functioning and establishment of the Common Market, thus justifying the recourse to Article 100.

These arguments make play with the transfrontier effects of advertising, distortions of conditions of competition and the free circulation of goods and services. If the protection of the consumer (and even the benefit of the general public) are also relied on, the justification nevertheless begins to envisage more precisely the particular requirements of legal basis chosen.

7. Council Directive of December 18, 1978 on the approximation of laws of Member States relating to the labelling, presentation and advertising of foodstuffs for sale to the ultimate consumer[37]

This Directive is based on Articles 100 and 227. The recourse to Article 100 is justified by reference to the disparities in the legislation in Member States impeding the free circulation of the products concerned and the creation of unequal conditions of competition. The adoption of the Directive would therefore, it is stated, contribute to the smooth functioning of the Common Market. There is no general reference to the objective of consumer protection, although this is stated to be an objective of the rules on labelling.

The reference to Article 227 seems to be slightly eccentric, but was presumably justified in the minds of the Community legislator by the fact that the Directive is stated not to apply to Greenland.

In general the justification of this Directive represents a considerable shift towards the position whereby measures are justified by reference to the specific requirements of the Article on which they are based and no longer by reference to a theory based on the objectives of the Treaty.

8. Proposed Directive relating to the approximation of the laws, regulations and administrative provisions of the Member States concerning consumer credit[38]

The proposal is based on Article 100. The preamble justifies the proposal on the ground of the wide differences which exist between

---

[37] O.J. 1979 L33/1.
[38] O.J. 1979 C80/4.

the consumer credit laws in force in the Member States, in particular as regards the degree of consumer protection in the various Member States and the opportunities for the consumer to obtain credit in another Member State. These differences affect the conditions of competition between creditors, the volume and nature of the credit sought and the purchase of goods and services and more generally the free movement of goods and services obtained on credit and thus the harmonious development of economic activities throughout the Community.

The preamble also makes reference to the preliminary programme and to various aspects in which the consumer needs protection, and asserts that for the reasons given the laws in force in the Member States directly affect the functioning of the Common Market.

9. Council Directive of June 19, 1979 on consumer protection in the indication of the prices of foodstuffs[39]

As adopted this Directive is based on Article 235. The preamble justifies the Directive by reference to the preliminary programme and also on the basis that: the indication of the selling price and the unit price of foodstuffs makes it easier for consumers to compare prices, thus increasing market transparency and consumer protection; and the rules in the Directive are needed for the purposes of consumer information and protection and further one of the objectives of the Community by contributing to the improvement of living conditions and the harmonious development of economic activities throughout the Community.

10. Council Decision of July 23, 1981 on the implementation of a pilot experiment relating to a Community system of information on accidents involving products outside spheres of occupational activities and road traffic[40]

This decision is based on Articles 213 and 235. The preamble justifies the decision by reference to the Preliminary Programme and on the grounds that: there should be special rules for informing consumers where products present a risk to their health or safety, improving their conditions of use or withdrawing them from the market; and the pilot experiment established by the decision appears necessary to achieve one of the Community's objectives as regards the protection and information of consumers.

No specific justification is given for combining Article 213 and 235, which seems to be in the nature of a political compromise rather than a well-thought out legal basis, particularly as recourse to Article 235 is only possible where no other legal basis is available.

---

[39] O.J. 1979 L158/19.
[40] O.J. 1981 L229/1.

11. Council Resolution of May 19, 1981 on a second programme of the European Economic Community for a consumer protection programme and information policy[41]

The justification is basically the same as that given for the first programme.

II. COMMENTARY

The proposals and the measures selected are those whose main emphasis is on consumer protection, as distinct from "internal market" Directives. The main aim of the latter is the removal of barriers to trade, even if there may be a secondary consumer protection element. The selection is, by necessity, a trifle arbitrary, especially as the consumer protection measures proposed on the basis of Article 100 place emphasis on the circulation of goods in their preambles wherever possible in order to show that the requirements of the legal basis are met.

The list contains measures of several distinct types as follows: an internal Commission Decision (1); Council Resolutions (2 and 11); proposals of the Commission which have not yet been adopted (3, 4, 5, 6 and 8); legal acts adopted by the Council (7, 9, 10).

Obviously the legal bases and justifications of these instruments vary accordingly to their nature. This has to be borne in mind when comparing them. In particular the approach of the Council is stricter than that of the Commission as regards the legal basis and justification. As, however, the Commission will, by force of circumstance, need to take into account what the Council will accept, proposals of the Commission may be expected to reflect the wording of precedents in the shape of previously adopted measures of consumer protection.

A certain evolution is discernable in the style of justification. This commences with a simple reliance on the objectives of the Treaty and the political green light, given at the Paris Summit Meeting of 1972, but later moves towards a more detailed justification with respect to the Article chosen as the legal basis. Where this is Article 100 a number of arguments are used, the most important being the distortion of conditions of competition and barriers to the free movement of goods and services, and others as appropriate such as cross boundary effects. The earlier emphasis on Article 100 seems to have shifted in favour of Article 235, although this choice is of course determined by the substantive content of the measure. The measure on unit pricing would, however, have been a candidate for Article 100.

The justifications for the measures based on Article 235 are noticeably more relaxed and indeed hark back to the original approach of the Commission. They seem to show a tendency on the part of the

[41] O.J. 1981 C133/1.

Council to recognise that protection of consumers is an aim of the Community. The double legal basis for the pilot experiment (point 10) seems, however, to indicate that Member States still feel a lot of uncertainty about consumer protection measures and seek to underpin Article 235 by other legal bases if possible.

The references in the preambles to the meeting of the Heads of State and Governments in 1972 and to the Preliminary Programme is in the nature of a political argument, as evidently a legal justification cannot be given on the basis of political declarations.

II

European Consumer Protection – A Progress Report

Ludwig Kraemer[1]

INTRODUCTION

When talking of legal aspects of consumer protection taken at the level of the European Economic Community, one should bear in mind that there are some features, which distinguish the EEC measures from action taken at a national level. The most striking distinctions include the following.

The EEC is not a nation-state

It does not have an overall, general competence, but is allowed to take action only to the extent which is indicated by the EEC Treaty. As the EEC Treaty speaks neither of a consumer policy nor of the necessity of protecting consumers' interests, any action aiming at strengthening or co-ordinating the interests of consumers needs a legal justification under the Treaty rules.

There is no public opinion at EEC level

In modern society, the participation of the media in the discussion of social aspects of society is of primary importance. This is particularly true for groups with diffused interests, minorities, the underprivileged, weak, etc. At least at Community level consumer interests are interests of a minority. They range from product safety to prices, from after-sales service to product information, from particularly weak groups (e.g. children, the elderly, the handicapped) to public interests (e.g. cost of health policy, environmental protection, functioning of competition). Unlike many other interest groups—farmers, producers of industrial products, insurance companies, banks—which are extremely well organised at EEC level and defend precise, specific interests, consumers often are not able to formulate their interests in a sufficiently precise manner. Thus they have difficulties in addressing the media, which are national and not EEC media and therefore pay more attention to the national interests of

---

[1] Deputy Head of Division, Directorate General for Environment, Consumer Protection and Nuclear Safety, Commission of the European Communities. The views expressed in this paper are those of the author and are not to be attributed to the Commission of the European Communities.

consumers than to their common EEC interests. In theory, public opinion is the best ally of consumers; as there is no public opinion at EEC level, this absence works to the detriment of consumer protection at EEC level.

The degree of organisation at EEC level remains low

In member countries political decisions are taken by majority votes of parliaments and governments are allowed to act, as long as they are allowed to do so by their parliaments. Community decisions are, at least in areas of consumer policy, taken unanimously, each Member State thus having a right of veto. Discussions are therefore prolonged until each Member State, or rather each administration, can agree. This, in the absence of pressure from public opinion, prolongs discussions and leads to results at the lowest common denominator where each Member State has its particular interests taken care of. Thus community legislation appears often to co-ordinate national legislation rather than to strengthen consumer protection.

Decision-making power in other groups is distributed in the same way. National parliaments have more "power" than the European Parliament; national farmers', producers', bankers', traders' or standardisation associations, trade unions or consumer organisations have generally more influence than the corresponding European organisations, which generally are financed, staffed and influenced in their policy by national interests. "Thinking federal" appears not to be a formula that applies to any relevant political, economic or social body at EEC-level.

These introductory remarks seem to suggest that action taken in the interest of consumers should best be left to national authorities and that the EEC should not deal with consumer protection. However, Article 2 of the Treaty expressly mentions that one of the aims of the EEC is an improvement in the standard of living. This applies to all citizens, not just to producers and traders. Therefore a European policy which aims at creating an internal market with free circulation of goods and services has also to assure an adequate protection of the health, safety and economic interests of individuals. It is inconceivable to establish a Common Market with harmonised rules of production and distribution, but with differing rules for health and safety requirements, marketing practices and access to justice. How can a product be safe in one part of the Common Market, but unsafe in another part, and yet circulate quite freely inside that Common Market? In fact, such a Common Market, which is "common" for producers and traders, but not for consumers, will not be able to exist, but will almost immediately split up again into different national markets. Either the EEC will be able to fix Community-wide rules for protecting the EEC consumers, or national measures, which legitimately assure this kind of protection, will question EEC rules on the establishment and functioning of the Common Market.

The Summit Conference of 1972 asked EEC institutions to take action in order to strengthen and co-ordinate measures to protect consumers. In 1973 the Commission set up the Environment and Consumer Protection Service which was, in 1981, transformed into a Directorate General. 1973 also saw the creation of the Consumers' Consultative Committee, an advisory body of, at present, 33 representatives from consumer interests. In 1975 a first, and in 1981 a second, Community programme for a consumer policy were adopted, which grouped consumer interests in five basic rights: the right of protection of consumer's health and safety, of his economic interests, the right of redress, help and assistance in judicial and para-judicial procedures, the right of information and education and the right to be heard in matters which affect consumers' interests. This progress report will broadly follow the lines traced by these five rights.

HEALTH AND SAFETY QUESTIONS

Little doubt exists as to the EEC competence to adopt legislation which affects consumers' health or safety. The main argument can be taken from Article 36 of the Treaty which gives Member States a competence to protect the life and health of citizens and to that end to restrict the free circulation of goods inside the EEC. However, it is the general opinion, frequently confirmed by the European Court of Justice, that Article 36 leaves only a residual competence to Member States and applies only to the extent that the EEC legislators have not yet adopted measures for the protection of health and safety.

There is no general, comprehensive Community safety legislation, nor is there a European Food and Drug Administration or Consumer Product Safety Commission, charged with checking the safety of consumer products. Several scientific committees are charged with defining EEC-wide rules of safety for specific areas, for instance the Scientific Committee for human consumption, for cosmetics, for pesticides, etc. However, the role of these committees is purely advisory; neither the Commission nor the Council of Ministers are in any way bound by their decisions. This applies likewise to the many other consultative committees set up to advise the Commission.[2]

There is no general framework-directive which fixes general rules as to product safety; nor can such general rules be derived directly from the EEC Treaty. It is true that the European Court of Justice stated, in its famous *Cassis de Dijon*[3] decision, that in absence of EEC legislation a product which was legally produced and marketed in one Member State could normally also be distributed in the other countries, even if national legislation in such countries required compliance with other rules.

---

[2] For a general overview see: "Commission, Consumer Representation at EEC level," (Brussels-Luxembourg 1982).
[3] Case 120/78, [1979] E.C.R. 649.

It is submitted, however, that this decision[4] does not apply to national rules regarding the health and safety of consumers. This seems to follow from a number of other decisions of the European Court: in the case *Biologische Producten*[5] the Court held that, in the absence of EEC rules, national authorities were entitled to decide whether or not to authorise the marketing of a pesticide on their territory, despite the fact that this pesticide had already received authorisation to be marketed in another Member State. In the *Nisine*[6] case the Court held that national authorities were allowed to prohibit the use of *Nisine* preservative on their territory, though that additive was in use in other Member States. And in the *Sandoz*[7] case the Court allowed national authorities to decide whether or not they would authorise the addition of vitamins to food products, though some Member States did allow such a practice.

It seems therefore that, in the absence of EEC rules, each Member State itself determines what kind of product it considers to be a risk for the health or safety of consumers. Up to now there is no general EEC licensing system for products nor is it intended to introduce one in future. A Commission proposal to introduce such an EEC-wide authorisation for pesticides[8] is still pending. New chemical substances have, however, to be registered and classified according to common EEC rules[9]; specific procedures aim at solving potential conflicts as to the risk assessment of a specific substance.

The central recognition of national authorisations is not very far advanced either. A recent attempt to introduce such a mutual recognition of national authorisations for pharmaceuticals was not successful.[10] Mutual recognition of car authorisations is still awaited, as this recognition will have to be accepted only after the adoption of the different Directives on car equipment, and three of these individual Directives are still pending before the Council.[11]

Many Directives lay down rules for composition, make-up, labelling and packaging of specific products and allow goods in conformity with these rules to circulate freely inside the EEC. A safeguard-clause enables Member States to stop the impact of products which, though conforming to EEC rules, present a health or safety risk. Special procedures at EEC level are fixed in order to eliminate eventual disagreements on the question whether or not the use of the safeguard-clause was justified. In the last resort the European Court of Justice will have to decide any such dispute.

Specific safety requirements at EEC level are fixed in the cosme-

[4] Discussed in detail by Jules Stuyck, *post*, p. 77.
[5] Case 272/80, [1981] E.C.R. 3279.
[6] Case 53/80, [1981] E.C.R. 409.
[7] Dec. of autumn 1983, not yet published.
[8] O.J. 1976 C 252/3.
[9] Dir. 67/548 J.O. 1967 L 196/1. Largely replaced by the "6th amendment"—Dir. 79/831 O.J. 1979 L 259/10.
[10] *Cf.* the Commission's proposal O.J. 1980 C 355/1; and Dir. 83/570 O.J. 1983 L 332/1.
[11] The adoption of these Directives is delayed because of Third World imports.

tics Directive[12] and in the "low-tension" Directive[13] which covers almost all electrical material for consumer use. Whereas the cosmetics Directive uses as a parameter that the product must be safe for "normal use," the low-voltage Directive indicates that electrical material has to be safe when used for its intended purposes when properly installed and maintained.[14] The Commission proposal on a Directive for toys[15] talks again of normal use or forseeable misuse. The different Directives on chemical substances and preparations[16] do not contain specific safety requirements.

The general regulation of products at EEC level has up to now been dealt with by only one Directive from 1976,[17] which so far has been amended five times. Each time specific products were prohibited or their use restricted. The Directive applies to chemicals only and requires a unanimous decision by the Council. As this procedure is very time-consuming and does not allow for a quick reaction to risks for consumers, which stem from products already on the market, the Commission recently reiterated its request for the adoption of rules which would allow such controls to be introduced by way of a speedy procedure.[18]

Other Directives provide for indirect prohibitions. This applies in particular to the different Directives for food additives,[19] which set up positive lists of additives that may be used by producers. Any additive that is not listed in those positive lists is prohibited at national level as well as at EEC level. For the time being Member States themselves decide which additive may be used in which product. Community legislation is to replace these national rules, but has not yet started and might well still take a very long time. The principle of positive lists is also to be retained for products which are destined to come into contact with food.[20]

The cosmetics Directive contains a list of substances which may not be contained in a cosmetic product (negative list); other substances may only be used up to certain limits. Such restrictions are also to be found in some other directives, in particular in the food sector. The Directive 79/117[21] prohibits the use of certain pesticides in the EEC and restricts the use of others.

---

[12] Dir. 76/768 O.J. 1976 L 262/169.
[13] Dir. 73/23 O.J. 1973 L 77/29.
[14] See also Hartley: "Consumer safety and the harmonisation of technical standards, the Low Voltage Directive" [1982] E.L.Rev. 55.
[15] O.J. 1983 C 203/1.
[16] Framework-Directive (ref. in n. 9) solvants O.J. 1973 L 189/7, pesticides O J 1978 L 206/13; paints and varnishes O.J. 1977 L 303/23.
[17] Dir. 76/769 O.J. 1976 L 262/201.
[18] Commission, doc. COM(83)556 fin. of September 26, 1983.
[19] Dir. of October 23, 1962 O.J., p. 2645 (colourants); Dir. 64/54 O.J. 1964 161 (preservatives); Dir. 70/357 O.J. 1970 L 157/31 (antioxidants); Dir. 74/329 O.J. 1974 L 189/1. (emulsifiants, etc.). All these Directives have been frequently amended since their adoption.
[20] Dir. 76/893 O.J. 1976 L 340/19; and Dir. 83/229 O.J. 1983 L 123/31.
[21] O.J. 1979 L 33/36.

The recall of dangerous products which are on the market is the subject of only one rule. Directive 75/319[22] requires Member States to introduce rules in order to recall pharmaceutical products which are harmful even when used according to the instructions. Member States have to report to an EEC committee on pharmaceutical products. The information is, however, not publicly available.

The Community does not operate a Home Accident Surveillance System. It agreed only to set up a pilot project on the subject, where participation is not compulsory.[23] So far, the EEC has not even taken a decision on the Commission proposal to set up an information system on dangers arising from products which are on the market.[24] Such a system, on a voluntary basis only, exists already in the food area; nothing however is published on its efficiency.[25]

Standardisation is of interest to consumers to the extent that it touches consumer products. And though standardisation goes far upon safety aspects—performance standards, quality standards, labelling standards are other examples—it is mentioned here because Community aspects of standardisation that are of interest to consumers relate almost exclusively to safety aspects.

The European standardisation organisations, CEN and CENELEC, include, as their member organisations, bodies from countries other than EEC countries. This might be one of the reasons why, until now, the elaboration of standards has been relatively slow. Since 1982 European consumer organisations may, by virtue of a gentlemen's agreement, send an observer to those working groups of CEN and CENELEC that are of interest to them.

European standards of relevance to consumers have mainly been elaborated in the area of electrical material, following the low-voltage Directive referred to earlier. That Directive is based on the legal concept of a "gliding reference to standards": products which bear a national EEC-wide recognised standardisation mark are supposed to comply with the electrical standards referred to by a general clause of the Directive and at the same time with the general safety requirements of the Directive. The different standards can be changed by international, European or national standardisation bodies without the EEC legislators intervening anew.

This very flexible approach allowed the EEC legislators to draft only a framework Directive and to leave all safety details to the standardisation organisations. As EEC legislation is progressing only slowly, the temptation is great to use the low-voltage Directive as a model for future legislation. From the consumer angle this procedure is acceptable, where the standards ensure sufficient safety; where consumer impact on the standardisation is sufficiently

---

[22] O.J. 1975 147/13.
[23] Dec. 81/623 O.J. 1981 L 229/1.
[24] O.J. 1979 C 321/7. (The decision was adopted on March 2, 1984, O.J. 1984 L70/16.)
[25] Apart from a reference in the 16th General Report of the Commission (1982), p. 92, that the system functions well.

assured; where precise monitoring systems—product control, accident data research, etc.—are made available; and where quick improvement of safety standards is assured, if necessary. These requirements are at present not fulfilled at EEC level.

In 1983, the EEC adopted a directive on information about planned national standardisation action.[26] The directive provides for a permanent, mutual exchange of information on work at national level, in order to allow either the EEC to take up the subject matter in question—in that case a standstill system works under the directive—or European or interested national standardisation bodies to assist at the meetings of the national organisation which started work. Although the direct consumer interest in this directive is small, the directive is likely to lead to considerably increased activity in the standardisation field at European level.

Looking at safety measures at EEC level in general, one is faced with dispersed, fragmented legislation which is not always coherent. Point by point, action can be explained by the fact that national action is only to be strengthened, not to be substituted. Common safety standards and common standards on risks are not frequent; Member States keep a broad competence on the approval for products to be put on the market as well as on the risk assessment. Food law is more advanced than other areas of safety law

Changes in the area of product safety arrive gradually. Technical standardisation at international level, European co-operation and the activities of trans-national companies will continue to increase the number of EEC measures on product safety. Whereas rules for the control of products—preventive and repressive controls—will mainly remain within the jurisdiction of Member States, the Community will gradually—*nolens volens*—move into EEC-wide reactions to safety risks—prohibitions, restrictions, warnings, recalls—and adopt legal instruments to create Community safety rules. Seen from the consumer side, there is much too little European-wide research, in the area of safety law, on its international and European ramifications and on the legal consequences thereof.

PRICES

The Rome Treaty does not give a general competence to the EEC on prices. The fixing of prices and their control form part of the general economic policy which Article 103 leaves generally in the hands of Member States.

Article 39 of the Treaty stipulates that the Common Agriculture Policy has to ensure that agricultural products reach consumers at reasonable prices. This article could suggest that retail prices for agricultural products should also be a subject of the CAP. However—one is tempted to say "fortunately"—it is generally admitted

---

[26] Dir. 83/183 O.J. 1983 L 109/8.

that CAP deals only with producers' prices; farmers' prices account for about 30 to 40 per cent. of the final retail price and thus the price policy of the EEC under the CAP has considerable impact on the consumer's budget, though it will not be discussed here.

For the rest, the EEC relies mainly on free competition as the market regulatory system. Articles 85 and 86 give relatively extensive power to the Commission in order to stop anti-competitive market behaviour. Article 86 in particular prohibits the abuse of a dominant position on the market, where this leads to excessive prices. Though the Court has expressly recognised the power of the Commission in its fight against excessive price fixing, it has laid down so many conditions for investigations into whether or not excessive prices are charged[27] that, *de facto*, the Commission is acting more than slowly because of lack of staff.

In its proposal for a regulation on selective distribution of cars,[28] the Commission suggested recently that selective distribution systems should only be allowed if the car prices before tax did not differ more than 12 per cent. inside the EEC (at present these differences go up to 40 per cent.) This part of the Commission's proposal has already been severely attacked by the car industries and it seems doubtful whether the price-clause will reappear in the final text of the regulation.

Another possibility for the EEC to intervene in the price area is that of Article 30 of the Treaty. This Article prohibits all quantitative restriction to the free circulation of goods as well as any measure having equivalent effect. The Court once had to decide whether national maximum prices constituted a measure having equivalent effect. In its decision[29] the Court confirmed the right of Member States to fix maximum prices, but indicated that prices could not be fixed in a way that made imports from other member countries virtually impossible. This was, according to the Court, particularly the case when the importer was unable to sell the products with a certain benefit which allowed him to cover transport and other import costs.

The Court fixed similar conditions for minimum prices fixed at national level[30] showing thus that it intended to question national price regulations on their compatibility with Article 30. At present, several cases are pending before the Court which concern national price rules with regard to pharmaceutical products. As regards price transparency, the EEC has a legitimate right to adopt measures in that area, thus increasing the opportunity for the consumer to compare prices of goods and services and buy wherever he wishes to do so. This price transparency is particularly important for border

---

[27] Case 27/76 *United Brands Co.* v. *Commission* [1978] E.C.R. 207 ("Chiquita Bananas"); Case 85/76 *Hoffman-La Roche AG* v. *Commission* [1979] E.C.R. 461.
[28] O.J. 1983 165/1.
[29] Case 13/77 *INNO* [1977] E.C.R. 2115.
[30] Case 82/77 *Netherlands* v. *Van Tiggele* [1978] E.C.R. 25.

regions, but not restricted to those. In fact under the present EEC rules[31] the consumer is entitled to buy goods up to 210 ECU in another country and import them free of tax; the Commission even suggested a gradual increase in this amount, up to 400 ECU. The Commission does not publish statistics on price differences from one country to the other. Price comparisons, though very limited in number and scope, are done by the European consumer organisation BEUC.[32]

As regards price labelling, the EEC adopted a Directive on price labelling and labelling the price per unit for food.[33] However, on the one hand this Directive allows for certain exemptions, in particular for small retail shops. On the other hand, standardised ranges of quantities, that are listed in a Community list of ranges, will most likely be exempted from the unit pricing obligation.[34]

At the end of 1983 the Commission submitted to the Council a Directive on price labelling and labelling per unit for products other than food.[35]

OTHER ECONOMIC INTERESTS OF CONSUMERS

This section will neither raise questions of EEC competence nor will it deal with marketing practices, unfair contract terms, product liability or misleading advertising; all these questions are being dealt with separately in this book.

Residual questions include insurance, consumer credit, tourism and legislation. In the area of consumer credit, the Commission submitted a proposal to the Council,[36] which was for more than four years filibustered by the European Parliament before Parliament delivered an opinion asking for approximately 60 amendments. The Commission is at present preparing an amendment to its own proposal.

The original proposal was to a considerable extent influenced by the British Consumer Credit Act 1974. Its main feature consists of covering, in one piece of legislation, the different types of credit arrangement, which up to now are frequently covered by different rules of law on the continent. It seems premature to give a detailed legal analysis of the proposal, as it is likely to be changed considerably in view of the request of the European Parliament on the one hand and during the discussions of the Council of Ministers on the other hand. It should however be mentioned that the Commission undertook at the request of the European Parliament to elaborate

---

[31] Dir. 69/169 J.O. 1969 L 133/6; last amendment by Dir. 82/443 O.J. 1982 L 206/35.
[32] See in particular the different publications for cars in BEUC News (Oct. 1981) 7, (Sept. 1982) 17, (June 1983) 25. Sometimes European surveys are published only by national consumer organisations.
[33] Dir. 79/581 O.J. 1979 L 158/19.
[34] See Council Resolution O.J. 1979 C 163/1.
[35] O.J. 1984, C 8/2.
[36] O.J. 1979 C 80/4.

Community-wide methods for calculating the effective rate of interest for consumer credit.[37]

As regards insurance, Articles 59 and following, in particular Article 61, paragraph 2 of the Treaty, provide for freedom of services in this area. In accordance with the general EEC programme on freedom of services, the freedom to provide insurance services was thought to necessitate compliance with three conditions: the realisation of the freedom of establishment for insurance companies, the approximation of insurance contract law and the mutual recognition and execution of judgments in insurance law matters. Whereas conditions one and three in the meantime have been largely fulfilled, condition two, which is of particular importance for consumers, is still lacking. A Commission proposal regarding insurance contract law, which was submitted to the Council in 1979,[38] is not yet adopted. And that proposal is far from ensuring the approximation of all relevant contract clauses, but limits itself to only some of the most important aspects.[39]

Consumers have often argued that the freedom to choose the law applicable to a contract, in particular to an insurance contract, should not be left to the discretion of the contracting parties, but that it should be the consumers' law which applies. For damage insurance the Commission, meeting a request of the European Parliament, has to a certain extent recognised this principle by suggesting[40] that, for mass risks, the rules of law of the member country on whose territory the risk is located should apply. The Council decision is still pending.

There is no particular EEC legislation concerning the protection of tourists. However, following a first discussion paper from the Commission on a tourism policy[41] Commission services are examining at present whether appropriate proposals should be made in the area of package holidays—a topic on which the European Consumer Law Group published an interesting document.[42]

In EEC tax law, the rules which are perhaps of greatest direct relevance to consumers are the rules on duty-free imports. By virtue of Directive 69/169[43] any consumer may, when travelling to another member country, upon his return import goods of a value up to 210 ECU (approximately £140) without paying any customs or taxes. The Commission has recently suggested that this amount be increased gradually up to 400 ECU,[44] which brings radios, tape recorders, smaller electrical household goods and other consumer durables sold in a neighbour country into the realm of consumers.

---

[37] O.J. 1983 C 68/9 and C 242/10.
[38] O.J. 1979 C 190/2.
[39] See recitals 6 and 7 of the proposal referred to in n. 38.
[40] O.J. 1976 C 32/2.
[41] Doc. COM(82) 385 final of July 1, 1982.
[42] 1979 *Journal of Consumer Policy* 314.
[43] See n. 31.
[44] O.J. 1983 C 114/7.

Price comparisons between different member countries can therefore be of particular interest to consumers, especially during the holiday periods of the year—and provided the results of the comparative surveys are published or otherwise made available to consumers.

CONSUMER INFORMATION

Numerous EEC directives deal with consumer information. They cannot all be examined here. The most relevant directive in the foodstuffs area is Directive 79/112[45] concerning the labelling of food, but referring also to food advertising. Food labelling (or advertising) must not mislead the consumer. Generally the following indications have to be given on the label: the designation of the product, a list of added substances, the quantity of the food, the peremption date, the name and address of a responsible person, place of origin, and eventually instructions for storage and handling and, where necessary, instructions for use.

The Directive provides for detailed rules on each of these principles, but enables Member States on many points to derogate. BEUC, the European consumer organisation, listed 40 of such derogations where the different Member States made different use of the permission to derogate.[46]

Consumer information on pharmaceutical products is governed by Directives 65/65[47] and 75/319.[48] It should be noted that Member States were unable to agree a mandatory introduction of an information leaflet to accompany each pharmaceutical product. Directive 75/319 leaves any such mandatory introduction to the discretion of the Member States, but indicates what minimum information such a leaflet would have to contain, should a member country decide to introduce it.

Consumer information on dangerous chemical substances and preparations is to a considerable extent regulated Community-wide by directives on dangerous substances,[49] solvents,[50] pesticides,[51] and paints and varnishes[52]; a general directive on all dangerous preparations is being prepared by the Commission. These directives introduce a system by virtue of which dangerous substances and preparations are being classified "toxic," "dangerous," "inflammable," "corrosive," etc. For most of these dangers symbols are introduced, which have to appear in black on an orange yellow background on the label and which must be accompanied, according to the specific danger from the product, by safety advice or pre-

---

[45] O.J. 1979 L 33/1.
[46] BEUC, "The EEC Directive on Food Labelling," BEUC/92/82 of July 20, 1982.
[47] J.O. 1965 p. 369.
[48] O.J. 1975 L 147/13.
[49] See n. 9.
[50] O.J. 1973 L 189/7, subsequently amended.
[51] O.J. 1978 L 206/13, subsequently amended.
[52] O.J. 1977 L 303/23, subsequently amended.

cautionary warnings. No symbols have so far been developed to indicate "dangerous for the environment," "carcinogenic," or "teratogenic." The symbol which was recently introduced in order to signal the presence of asbestos[53] completely departs from the general warning system, just showing an "a" letter plus a warning phrase. Neither the dangerous chemicals Directives nor that on asbestos require the warnings on the labels to be written in the consumer's language, but allow Member States to make the consumer's language mandatory.

Consumer information on cosmetics is regulated by the Cosmetics Directive,[54] as subsequently amended. The presence of dangerous substances in cosmetics is not indicated by a warning to the consumer, but generally only by the requirement to state the name of the dangerous substance on the label. Otherwise the composition of the product need not be given on the label.

Origin marking of products is generally not considered to be part of consumer information. The foodstuffs labelling rule—the origin has to be indicated, if otherwise the consumer could be misled about the real origin of the product—appears to express a general philosophy. In 1980 the Commission introduced a proposal on origin marking of textiles,[55] but withdrew it quickly and replaced it by a proposal for a Regulation on textile origin marking for third world imports.[56] The proposal, based on Article 113 of the Treaty, is rather to be seen in the context of the Multifibre arrangement in the framework of GATT than as a piece of consumer information. This view is confirmed by the fact that the Commission introduced court action against the United Kingdom which adopted national rules on the origin marking of some products.

Quality information for consumers hardly appears in EEC legislation. Directives on energy consumption of electrical household products have been intiated, but only a framework Directive and one specific Directive on energy consumption of electric ovens have been adopted up to now.[57] It seems as if the effort in this area is not continuing. On noise labelling, the Commission introduced proposals on noise labelling of household appliances and of lawn mowers, [58] but these have not yet been adopted.

OTHER MATTERS

Of the other EEC legislation, which may be of interest to consumers, only a few items can be mentioned here. There are several environ-

---

[53] Dir. 83/478 O.J. 1983 L 263/33.
[54] For. ref., see n. 12.
[55] O.J. 1980 C 294/3.
[56] O.J. 1982 C 93/11.
[57] Dir. 79/530 O.J. 1979 L 145/1 (framework Directive); Dir. 79/351 O.J. 1979 L 145/7 (electric ovens).
[58] O.J. 1982 C 181/1 (household appliances); O.J. 1979 C 86/9 (lawn mowers).

ment Directives closely affecting consumers, in particular the Directives on the quality of bathing water[59] and drinking water,[60] on lead in petrol[61] and on air pollution.[62] Two international Conventions, on the enforcement of judgments[63] and on the law applicable to contractual obligations,[64] will have considerable influence on the individual consumer inside the EEC, though their legal nature—Community instruments or international law—is the subject of many a scholar's dispute. The two proposals on trade mark law[65] will also influence considerably the consumer's position.

CONCLUSION

The EEC is a philosophy in action, rather than a once and for all static body, in which rules are elaborated under a preconceived programme which remains valid for a long time. Where trade and industry organise themselves at European or even international level, consumers cannot hope to receive an adequate amount of protection or information by local, regional or national steps. This phrase remains true under a Marxist concept of economy as well as under a "free market" concept.

EEC measures to protect or inform consumers, which are mostly undertaken with legal instruments, are scattered, incomplete and slow. They achieve progress inch by inch, not by way of big steps. In this they do not differ from other measures adopted by the EEC—in industrial policy, development policy, regional policy, fiscal policy, and so forth.

---

[59] O.J. 1976 L 31/1.
[60] O.J. 1975 L 194/34.
[61] O.J. 1978 L 197/19.
[62] O.J. 1980 L 229/30.
[63] O.J. 1983 C 97/2, (amended version).
[64] O.J. 1980 L 266/1.
[65] O.J. 1980 C 351/5.

III

Proposed EEC Directive on Misleading and Unfair Advertising

S. H. Freedman[1]

The sole legislative proposal on advertising currently under consideration by the EEC Council of Ministers concerns misleading and unfair advertising. A draft Directive was submitted to the Council by the Commission in 1978.[2] Following the usual procedure under Article 100 of the EEC Treaty it was sent to the European Parliament and to the Economic and Social Committee for their opinion. Both of them gave a broad measure of support to the draft Directive and suggested certain improvements. The Commission amended the text accordingly in July, 1979.[3] Since then it has been discussed in a working group of the Member States. When it has been unanimously agreed, it will be adopted by the Council and passed into national law.

Although it figures as a priority for action in both the First and the Second EEC Consumer Programmes, the proposal has wider implications than the benefit of consumers. Article 1 indicates that it is also intended to protect the interests of people carrying on a trade, business or profession. Indeed, when the proposal was first prepared, it was conceived in terms of unfair competition law.

UNFAIR COMPETITION

Laws for the protection of the ecomonic interests of consumers and laws against unfair competition are very often opposite sides of the same coin. A trader who successfully deceives consumers by misleading advertising at the same time takes an unfair competitive advantage over other traders. Consequently, the protection of consumers against misleading or unfair advertising also benefits ethical and law-abiding traders by ensuring fair competition. People who attack consumer legislation by alleging that it imposes an undue burden on commerce and industry often overlook this point.

---

[1] Head of Division, Directorate-General for Environment, Consumer Protection and Nuclear Safety, Commission of the European Communities. The views expressed in this paper are those of the author and are not to be attributed to the Commission of the European Communities.
[2] O. J. 1978 C 70/4.
[3] O. J. 1979 C 194/3.

The proposed Directive is intended to harmonise the laws of the EEC Member States. Any attempt to span the unfair competition law of Britain and the continental Member States is bound to be fraught with difficulty, because the common law has no general concept of unfair competition, whereas the continental systems do. For example, German law has an Act against unfair competition dating from 1909 (Gesetz gegen den unlauterem Wettbewerb (1909)). Section 1 states that any person who in the course of a business activity for the purposes of competition commits an act contrary to honest practices ("guten Sitten") may be enjoined from such practices.

This formulation is to be found in the Paris Convention of 1883.[4] The United Kingdom and Ireland have both ratified the Paris Convention. However, their law has developed in a less comprehensive fashion than that of the continental EEC Member States. It is somewhat difficult to understand why this should have happened. One possible explanation is that the common law countries take a narrow view of the Paris Convention, holding that it does not deal with unfair competition in a vacuum, but is concerned only with such matters as patents, trade marks and designs, so that unfair competition has to be considered in the context of industrial property rights. The issue does not appear to have been raised in a British or Irish case; however, it arose in a Canadian case, *McDonald* v. *Vapour Canada Ltd.* (22 C.P.R. 1), where it was linked with a constitutional issue. The "narrow view" prevailed, summarised in the headnote as follows:

> "Sweeping as the text of the Paris Convention, 1883, might appear, it does not afford any support to s.7(*e*) of the Trade Marks Act when there has been a finding that respondent's industrial property (other than unfair competition) as such has not been invaded. Article 10 bis of the Convention must be read in the context of the other articles of the Convention, none

---

[4] *Art. 10*bis *(Unfair Competition).*
   (1) The countries of the Union are bound to assure to nationals of such countries effective protection against unfair competition.
   (2) Any act of competition contrary to honest practices in industrial or commercial matters constitutes an act of unfair competition.
   (3) The following in particular shall be prohibited:
      1. all acts of such a nature as to create confusion by any means whatever with the establishment, the goods, or the industrial or commercial activities, of a competitor;
      2. false allegations in the course of trade of such a nature as to discredit the establishment, the goods, or the industrial or commercial activities, of a competitor;
      3. indications or allegations the use of which in the course of trade is liable to mislead the public as to the nature, the manufacturing process, the characteristics, the suitability for their purpose, or the quantity, of the goods.

of which deals with the contractual relationship between employer and employee."[5]

DIFFERENT EUROPEAN APPROACHES

The difference of approach between the common law countries and the continental EEC Member States has led to considerable variations in what is allowed by way of advertising. For example, in Britain comparative advertising, naming competitors and their products, is lawful. On the Continent it is illegal almost everywhere. Another example is advertising which denigrates a competitor. An extreme example would be: "Do not buy bread from X the baker, because he beats his wife."[6] On the Continent such advertising could be attacked on the grounds of unfair competition: whether the baker beats his wife is totally extraneous to the process of making and selling bread. In the common law countries, however, no action for defamation or injurious falsehood will lie if the statement is true, and there is no comparable action for unfair competition.

Although substantial differences exist between EEC Member States in the laws and regulations relating to advertising, the House of Lords Scrutiny Committee, which reported on the proposed Directive, considered that they do not justify the adoption of a measure to establish a common basis of understanding and recourse.[7] The Committee held there was no evidence of an effect on the Common Market.

EFFECTS ON THE COMMON MARKET

And yet the Common Market is intended to be a market without barriers to trade, a unity. There are within the Common Market at

---

[5] The case was concerned with the validity of a covenant in restraint of trade. Section 7 of the Trade Marks Act 1953 provides as follows:
"7. No person shall
  (a) make a false or misleading statement tending to discredit the business, wares or services of a competitor;
  (b) direct public attention to his wares, services or business in such a way as to cause or be likely to cause confusion in Canada, at the time he commenced so to direct attention to them, between his wares, services or business and the wares, services or business of another;
  (c) pass off other wares or services as and for those ordered or requested;
  (d) make use, in association with wares or services, of any description that is false in a material respect and likely to mislead the public as to
    (i) the character, quality, quantity or composition,
    (ii) the geographical origin, or
    (iii) the mode of the manufacture, production or performance
  of such wares or services; or
  (e) do any other act or adopt any other business practice contrary to honest industrial or commercial usage in Canada."

[6] Given the questions of taste and decency involved, whether such advertising could be published, except by private distribution, is somewhat doubtful.

[7] Report of the Select Committee on the European Communities on Misleading Advertising (R/511/78) p. IX, para 28.

present 10 Member States, each with its own system of advertising control. Rules vary, sometimes according to the subject matter of the advertisement, sometimes also according to the medium—be it press or television. None of this facilitates the marketing of goods or services in the Common Market. For example, a British firm wanting to use comparative advertising to promote the sale of its products on the Continent would be inviting an action on the grounds of unfair competition, even though it may have legitimately and successfully used this technique in the domestic British market, and invested heavily in developing its advertising campaign.

Admittedly, not all advertising crosses frontiers. Some is purely local. On the other hand, there is a good deal of cross-frontier advertising. Advertisements cross frontiers on the packaging of goods. It may be broadcast across frontiers through the medium of radio or television, or in the press. In such cases differences between the advertising regulations of the EEC Member States can complicate the marketing process, and may go so far as to disrupt the free circulation of goods and the availability of services in the Common Market.

It is only comparatively recently that this type of case has come before a European Court of Justice. In *Commission* v. *France*[8] the court was concerned with an express prohibition on advertising. The parties accepted that a ban of this kind can be a quantitative restriction within the meaning of Article 30 of the EEC Treaty and therefore void, unless justified under Article 36.

In cases under Article 30, the Court of Justice has for many years recognised the impossibility of proving a negative. It does not require quantitative evidence that imports from one Member State into another have been reduced, or did not take place, in order to prove that an obstacle exists to the free circulation of goods.[9] In *Commission* v. *France* the facts of the case showed that regulations introduced by the French Government to govern the advertising of alcoholic drinks discriminated against foreign products such as whisky or gin, while permitting wine-based products to be advertised. It was argued by the French Government that the regulations were justified for the protection of consumer health, on the grounds that whisky and gin are aperitifs. They tend to be drunk before meals and enter the blood stream more rapidly than digestifs consumed after meals. The Court recognised that alcoholism was a problem in France. Nevertheless, it considered the action taken was out of all proportion.

However, in condemning the regulations the court stated the issue as follows:

[8] [1980] E. C. R. 2299.
[9] *Procureur du Roi* v. *Dassonville* [1974] E. C. R. 837:
 "All trading rules enacted by Member States which are capable of hindering directly or indirectly, actually or potentially, intra-Community trade are to be considered as measures having an effect equivalent to quantitative restrictions."

"As a preliminary point it should be observed that there is no dispute between the parties on whether a restriction on freedom of advertising for certain products may constitute a measure having an effect equivalent to a quantitative restriction within the meaning of Article 30 of the Treaty. *Although such a restriction does not directly affect imports it is however capable of restricting their volume owing to the fact that it affects the marketing prospects for the imported products.* The issue in point is therefore whether the prohibitions and restrictions on advertising laid down by the French legislation place a handicap on the importation of alcoholic products from other Member States."[10]

Thus, where national rules on advertising interfere with the operation of the Common Market, the Court of Justice may condemn them under Article 30 as measures equivalent to quantitative restrictions, if they adversely affect the marketing prospects of imported products.

Cassis de Dijon

This judgment is consistent with the position adopted by the Court in the earlier case of *Rewe* v. *Bundesmonopolverwaltung für Branntwein*[11] which was concerned with a German marketing regulation prohibiting the sale of the French liqueur, Cassis. The German Government maintained before the court that the regulation was justified by consumer protection. It was designed to avoid proliferation on the national market of beverages with a low alcoholic content, which might more easily induce a tolerance towards alcohol than would stronger drinks. Another argument was that consumers would be deceived by the marketing of a liqueur with a lower alcoholic content than the liqueurs normally sold in Germany, because the alcohol content determines price to a large extent.

The Court dismissed the German Government's case. An extremely wide range of alcoholic products were already available on the German market. Furthermore, strong drinks may be consumed in a diluted form. As to the second line of argument, the Court pointed out that the relevant information could be conveyed by adequate labelling. The Court ruled that, in the absence of Community measures, Member States were entitled to regulate the marketing of products *inter alia* to protect consumers. Nevertheless, if such measures hinder the free circulation of goods between Member States, they will infringe the rules of Community law unless three conditions are fulfilled. First, the rules in question must be necessary in order to satisfy mandatory requirements. Secondly, they must serve a purpose in the general interest. Thirdly, they must be essential for the achievement of such a purpose. These conditions were

---

[10] Emphasis added.
[11] [1979] E. C. R. 649, generally called the *Cassis de Dijon* case.

not fulfilled in the *Cassis de Dijon* case. The case did not directly concern advertising. However, the reasoning of the German government in the *Cassis de Dijon case* could equally well have been used in an action for unfair competition by German producers or distributors of liqueurs against the advertising of Cassis.

Satellite advertising

The advent of satellites dramatically emphasises the case for the Directive. Television advertising will become increasingly more international than it is at present. As a result, it will become increasingly difficult to maintain purely national standards, especially because of the inevitable overlap of reception across the borders of the transmitting state. International problems require international solutions. The proposed Directive is the basis for agreement at the EEC level, not just for television but for other media too.

Once the position is agreed for the EEC as a whole, it will at one and the same time strengthen the Community's hand in negotiations with non-member states. The problem does not stop at the borders of the Community. Satellite transmissions from outside the Community could be used to circumvent the rules which apply within it. Some non-member states would welcome the advertising revenue, and advertisers would also be under pressure—even tempted—to use facilities affording greater freedom with regard to advertising techniques and the products which may be advertised.

CONTENT OF THE DIRECTIVE

So much for the need for the Directive. To turn to its content: the Directive is very broad in scope. It covers all forms of advertising in all media. It defines both misleading and unfair advertising, and also proposes certain remedies. The definition of misleading advertising is general. This contrasts with the situation under the law of the United Kingdom. There are many statutes which relate to the control of advertising. However, the Trade Descriptions Act 1968 is the main statutory provision. It is wide ranging, but specific in approach, providing for a number of criminal offences in precise terms. Implementation of the Directive would require a general duty not to deceive in advertising to be introduced in the United Kingdom. This would go beyond fraudulent claims.

The standards proposed are objective. Misleading and unfair advertising may be prohibited even without proof of fault or of prejudice. For example, a complainant will not have to show that an advertiser intended to mislead or was negligent. It will be enough to show that the effect of the advertisement is misleading, *i.e.* that the consumer is likely to be deceived whether or not there was an intention to deceive or negligence on the part of the advertiser. Nor need the complainant prove loss resulting from the advertisement. Misleading and unfair advertising are inherently likely to cause loss and should be restrained to prevent such loss occurring. The Directive does not cover damages for loss caused by misleading or unfair advertising. The aim is to restrain those types of advertising abuse. Under the Directive an advertisement may be misleading if it is false or partially false. It may also be misleading if, having regard to its total effect, including its presentation, it misleads or is likely to mislead consumers. Another case defined as misleading is where an advertisement omits material information. An example of an advertisement which transgressed in this way is one which appeared some years ago in the national press in Britain. It was an advertisement for a car, which was an ordinary, production model. However, the advertisement claimed that it accelerated faster in top gear from 30 to 50 m.p.h. than either the Porsche 911S or the Ferrari Dino, both high-performance sports cars. It omitted to mention that the car advertised had four gears and the others had five.

Another example was an advertisement for a well-known brand of paraffin sold as fuel for heaters. The advertisement claimed that it would not rust the can in which it was kept. That claim is true—just as the claim in the car advertisement was true—in itself. What the paraffin advertisement omitted was that *no paraffin*, whatever the brand, will rust the can in which it is kept. Paraffin is a product of petroleum and does not induce rusting. However, the advertisement raises a false expectation on the part of the consumer that the product in question has some special advantage over competing products.

Whereas the definition of misleading advertising is concerned with the information given by advertising, unfair advertising is concerned with the way in which advertising may manipulate the judgment of consumers. Thus, the definition of unfair advertising in the Directive identified a number of abuses, some of which are not currently the subject of control by a public authority in the United Kingdom, nor capable of being enforced by an action to defend a private interest. For example, the definition covers advertising which abuses or unjustifiably arouses sentiments of fear, or which abuses the trust, credulity or lack of experience of a consumer.[12]

Comparative Advertising

The Directive deals specifically with comparative advertising in Article 4. It states:

> "Comparative advertising shall be allowed as long as it compares material and verifiable details and is neither misleading nor unfair."

---

[12] See Postscript, p. 51.

This provision is different in nature from the rest of the Directive. It is positive. It says that comparative advertising shall be lawful, whereas the rest of the Directive is concerned with restraining advertising abuses. Of course, advertisers are not compelled to make comparisons, in the sense of naming competitors or their products. However, the intention is that they should in future be free to do so, subject to the qualifications stated.

Some advertisers are averse to this form. Mentioning a competitor or his product in an advertisement is still publicity for the competitor, even if the advertiser's intention is to boost his own products or services. On the other hand, there can be no doubt that (if it is well done) comparative advertising is very good advertising, especially from the consumer's point of view. It provides the consumer with information which may be extremely useful in enabling him to make a rational choice in the market place. Such information can promote market transparency and intensify competition, by giving advertisers an opportunity to explain to the public the competitive features of their products or services in a very direct way. This was the reasoning which led the Commission to conclude that comparative advertising should be declared admissible under certain conditions.[13]

An important issue relating to comparative advertising concerns trade marks. It is almost inevitable that an advertisement which refers to competitors, or competing products, will mention without authorisation a trade mark owned or used by that competitor. Is this an infringement of the trade mark? The underlying purpose of trade mark law is to prevent confusion on the part of consumers (using the term in its widest sense to mean a trade consumer as well as the ultimate consumer) caused by the employment of an identical or similar mark in an unauthorised fashion. However, this is not the case with comparative advertising. The advertiser who mentions a competitor's trade marks does not want to create confusion on the part of consumers. His purpose is quite the opposite. He makes the comparison in order to point out the advantages of his own product. He wants the consumer to distinguish clearly between his products and competitive products, because he wants the consumer to purchase the products which he, the advertiser, puts on the market.

The Directive was formulated with this problem in mind. If comparative advertising is to be lawful then, should there be a conflict

---

[13] Continental Member States of the EEC have been traditionally hostile to comparative advertising. Nevertheless, the position is developing. France has been actively considering whether to legitimise comparative advertising. In Switzerland, outside the EEC, there is also a draft proposal for a law against unfair competition, which would legitimate such advertising provided it is not inaccurate, misleading, denigratory or parasitic. (Message à l'appui d'une loi fédérale contre la concurrence déloyale (LCD) du 18 mai 1983, No. 83.038).

with the trade mark law of Member States, it is to be resolved in favour of permitting advertisers to mention their competitors trade marks for the purpose of a comparison. The impact on British law is probably to require Section 4(1) of the Trade Marks Act, 1938 to be repealed.

REMEDIES

As to remedies,[14] the approach embodied in the Directive is that prevention is better than a cure. It requires Member States to have effective laws so that misleading or unfair advertising can be withdrawn from circulation. It also requires deception of the public to be remedied, if appropriate, by corrective statements and also by the publication of the decisions of courts or administrative authorities. Such procedures should be swift and inexpensive. To remedy the harm done by misleading or unfair advertising speed is of the essence.

The Directive does not specify how it is to be implemented. The measures it contains could be incorporated in criminal, administrative or civil law at the discretion of the Member States. Lord Diplock, in the debate on the Directive which took place in the House of Lords,[15] described these provisions as a hotch-potch of rules lifted bodily from Romano-Germanic systems of law and entirely inappropriate in Britain. And yet other common law countries have adopted these rules. They operate in Australia, Canada and the United States. Most countries have a mixed approach, using criminal and administrative measures, as well as permitting civil suits. That is true of the U.K. The question is more one of the balance between the different approaches.

There are a limited number of measures which can be taken to counteract misleading or unfair advertising. It can be made a criminal offence. However, this approach has a number of disadvantages. The sanction is limited to the specific advertisement. It does not relate to future conduct. Secondly, if a fine is imposed, it may be regarded as part of the cost of the advertising campaign. If enforcement is entrusted to local authorities, they may be reluctant to attack the national media. There is the attendant disadvantage that the decisions of local courts may vary considerably from one part of the country to another, so that no coherent standards apply.

An injunction goes a step further in prohibiting the advertising complained of, not only at the time of the decision to grant the injunction, but for all future occasions as well. It suffers from the disadvantage that the damage may already be done by the time the order issues. Out of that consideration is born the idea of corrective advertising, whereby the advertiser is compelled to correct the mis-

---

[14] Art. 5.
[15] *Hansard* Vol. 396 No. 12 of November 28, 1978.

leading or unfair impression created by the infringing advertisement.

Corrective Advertisements

It has been questioned whether the people misled by the original advertisement will see the correction; but it would be wrong to let the best be the enemy of the good. Some of those people will see the correction, perhaps a great many. It will, therefore, have at least some utility and, perhaps, a very great deal. A parallel exists with the publication of apologies under the Defamation Act 1952. The apology will not be seen by everybody who read the original defamatory statement, but the solution is the best available in practical terms.

It has also been said that judges would find it difficult to draft corrective advertisements, and have no power to compel a newspaper—if not a party to the action—to publish a corrective advertisement. However, on payment, newspapers probably would publish corrections, just as they publish legal notices, for example, concerning bankruptcies or company liquidations. As to the difficulties this would cause judges, in practice a corrective statement would probably be drafted and agreed by Counsel appearing in the case. If it were not agreed, the judge would intervene and make an appropriate order. Should that be difficult in the circumstances of a particular case, then it might not be a suitable case for the publication of a corrective statement.

This type of provision exists in other common law jurisdictions. For example, in Australia, under section 80A(*b*) of the Federal Trade Practices Act 1974, the Australian courts can order corrective advertisements. And if Australian judges are capable of exercising this power, then probably British judges are too. Experience in the United States, however, has shown that corrective advertising can produce unforeseen results, even increasing the sales attributable to the original misleading or unfair advertisement. In France, the only EEC Member State where this remedy exists, corrective advertising has hardly been used at all.

Nevertheless, it is a useful weapon in the armoury of those who will be responsible for adjudicating on advertising issues, to be used at their discretion. In the USA swingeing orders have been made. The defendants in the *Listerine* case, for example, were ordered to state in their advertising that:

> "Contrary to prior advertising of Listerine, Listerine will not prevent or cure colds or sore throats, and Listerine will not be beneficial in the treatment of cold or sore throats."

The order provided that they were to spend the equivalent of their advertising budget for Listerine for 10 years to communicate that message.

The consequences for the advertiser could be very considerable financially and in terms of loss of goodwill. It is interesting to note that the Federal Trade Practices Act 1974 in Australia, while admitting the remedy of corrective advertising, imposes a limit on the expenditure which can be ordered.

Class actions

The original draft of the Commission's Directive submitted to the Council of Ministers in 1978 proposed that the courts should have the power to apply these remedies on the complaint of persons affected and of associations with a legitimate interest. The reference to associations is to provide a means whereby consumers can collectively secure redress, particularly in cases where the interest of the individual is insufficient to warrant an action, or where the individual has insufficient knowledge or experience to identify misleading advertisements.

France, the Federal Republic of Germany and the Netherlands have all given consumer associations the right to proceed at law against misleading advertising. However, in the United Kingdom this right of access to the law courts for consumer associations would involve the introduction of "class actions," or more accurately, a very considerable extension to the existing rules.

Even in the case of "persons affected," the law is still narrower than the Directive would require, because of the lack of a concept of unfair competition. Where a firm deceives the public, its competitors cannot sue unless their goodwill is directly affected. In the case of the advertisement for "Brand X—the paraffin which will not rust the can," competitors of the advertiser would have been unable to take action qua competitor to restrain the deception, even though it created an unfair competitive advantage.

PASSING-OFF—WARNINK CASE

The nearest that English law comes to creating a right of action for unfair competition is in cases of passing-off, a branch of the law which saw a notable development in the *Warnink* case.[16] The plaintiffs in that case sued to restrain the sale as "advocaat" of a concoction which was in fact "egg flip." They had no proprietary right in the name "advocaat," whether individually or jointly with other producers. However, they were associated in the mind of the public with "advocaat." Warnink succeeded in their action. The actual or potential injury to their goodwill gave them sufficient interest on which to base a cause of action.

In his Opinion, Lord Diplock pointed to a trend requiring increasingly high standards of honesty in the market:

---

[16] *Warnink* v. *Townend* [1979] 2 All E. R. 927 at p. 933.

"The market in which the action for passing off originated was no place for the mealy mouthed: advertisements are not on affidavit; exaggerated claims by a trader about the quality of his wares, assertions that they are better than those of his rivals, even though he knows this to be untrue, have been permitted by the common law as venial "puffing" which gives no cause of action to a competitor even though he can show that he has suffered actual damage in his business as a result.

Parliament, however, beginning in the 19th century has progressively intervened in the interests of consumers to impose on traders a higher standard of commercial candour than the legal maxim caveat emptor calls for, by prohibiting under penal sanctions misleading descriptions of the character or quality of goods; but since the class of persons for whose protection the Merchandise Marks Acts 1887 and 1953 and even more rigorous later statutes are designed are not competing traders but those consumers who are likely to be deceived, the Acts do not themselves give rise to any civil action for breach of statutory duty on the part of a competing trader even though he sustains actual damage as a result: *Cutler* v. *Wandsworth Stadium Ltd.*[17]; and see *London Armoury Co. Ltd.* v. *Ever Ready Co. (Great Britain) Ltd.*[18] Nevertheless the increasing recognition by Parliament of the need for more rigorous standards of commercial honesty is a factor which should not be overlooked by a judge confronted by the choice whether or not to extend by analogy to circumstances in which it has not previously been applied a principle which has been applied in previous cases where the circumstances although different had some features in common with those of the case which he has to decide. Where over a period of years there can be discerned a steady trend in legislation which reflects the view of successive Parliaments as to what the public interest demands in a particular field of law, development of the common law in that part of the same field which has been left to it ought to proceed on a parallel rather than a diverging course."

It is difficult to state exactly where the law stands today, for the door does seem to have been left open for the development of a more general tort of unfair competition out of the passing-off action.

ADMINISTRATIVE CONTROL

Very deep issues of policy have been raised by the proposal of class actions for consumer organisations, and the extension—at least, in the United Kingdom, if not in most other EEC Member States—of the rights of competitors to restrain unfair competitive advantages.

---

[17] [1949] A. C. 398.
[18] [1941] 1 All E. R. 364.

However, after the European Parliament's resolution on the Directive it was amended in a way which enables the British government to avoid having to grasp the nettle. The amended Directive introduced, as an alternative to recourse before the courts of law, the notion of control by an administrative authority empowered to apply the remedies called for by the Directive. The amendment reflected the reality of the situation actually prevailing in a number of EEC Member States. For example, in France, the Netherlands and the United Kingdom television advertising is controlled by administrative authorities. In Denmark the Consumer Ombudsman is responsible for taking action against advertising abuses under the Marketing Act. There is clearly a place for the exercise of public responsibility in maintaining honest practices in advertising. It would be less effective if left entirely to private initiatives.

These issues were discussed some years ago in a working group established by the Department of Trade under the Chairmanship of the then Deputy Secretary, John Burgh. Their report recommended extending the powers of the Office of Fair Trading to ensure compliance with the law, as a back-up to the self-regulatory activities of the Advertising Standards Authority. The OFT would be invested with powers to seek an injunction from the courts in appropriate cases. Thus, the United Kingdom will comply with the Directive by choosing an administrative solution.

Nevertheless, the Commission wants to see the courts have the last word, and Article 5 of the Directive has a final paragraph providing for the possibility of judicial review of administrative proceedings.

In conclusion, it should be noted that the Directive is intended to achieve a minimal harmonisation. Member States may take more stringent measures to protect consumers and enterprises than those in the Directive. This is bound to be so. The Directive does not touch upon the question of damages for misrepresentation or unfair competition, so that it inevitably has a limited application. In addition, some Member States already have very stringent provisions in their law. They cannot be expected to reduce their standards of consumer protection in the interests of harmonisation of laws.

POSTSCRIPT

Several months have elapsed between the date when this paper was given and its publication. In that time the Ministers responsible for consumer affairs in the 10 EEC Member States have met as a Council for the first time ever to discuss, *inter alia*, the proposed Directive on misleading and unfair advertising. In an endeavour to achieve agreement, the Council has simplifed and reduced the issues involved by deciding to omit unfair and comparative advertising from the proposal. Let us hope that this fresh initiative will result in its speedy adoption.

IV

Self-Regulation in Advertising—Some Observations from the Advertising Standards Authority

Peter Thomson[1]

INTRODUCTION

In each of the various drafts, official and unofficial, through which the European Community's proposed Directive on Advertising has passed since 1975, there has been an acceptance, with varying degrees of enthusiasm, of the fact that, in most of the Member States of the Community, some part of the burden of protecting the consumer from advertisements which are misleading or unfair now falls on self-regulatory mechanisms.

Despite this, the application of self-regulation to the control of commercial activity still strikes many observers, familiar enough with the notion in the liberal professions, as something of an oddity—and an unwelcome oddity at that. The attitude expressed by the European Community Law Group in their recent report[2]—in which they recommend the Commission to have as little to do with self-regulation as a means of securing consumer protection as it can—is typical. Yet what ECLG offer by way of justification for their advice is not a demonstration of the proven failure of self-regulation but an essentially theoretical discussion of what are said to be its disadvantages in which it never becomes clear whether one is being invited to dismiss the idea because it cannot work, because it does not work or because it does work but, so far as the authors are concerned, has unwelcome consequences.

Clearly the time has come for some attempt to clarify what self-regulation is and is not; some effort to show how it can operate to supplement rather than to supplant alternative and particularly legal modes of control; and some assessment of the scale of the challenge which it confronts in the control of advertising—and of its success in meeting that challenge.

---

[1] Director-General, Advertising Standards Authority.
[2] *Report on non-legislative means of consumer protection*, ECLG/156/82 of November 19, 1982.

A DEFINITION OF SELF-REGULATION

Let me begin by attempting to define what I mean by self-regulation. In essence, self-regulation consists of the regulation of an activity on a co-operative basis by those engaged in it; from which it follows that if entitlement to participate in the process of regulation does not principally derive from participation in the activity regulated, the process should not be described as self-regulation. Systems of ostensible self-regulation are sometimes subject to oversight by an outside body; whether such systems are truly self-regulatory will depend upon the nature and extent of the powers of the supervisory body. If, for example, the rules to be observed are laid down, or can be changed, solely (or even mainly) at the discretion of the outside body, then the system should not be described as self-regulatory. That a body of rules is called a "code of practice" does not necessarily entail compliance with those rules being secured by self-regulation. Indeed, compliance with codes of practice which emerge from, or through consultation with, governments and international bodies is frequently secured by legal means. The point is of some importance, since criticism of self-regulation as I have defined it is, as one can see from the ECLG paper, sometimes misdirected in consequence of this confusion.

The "self" in self-regulation refers to the body corporate, and not to the individual practitioner. Thus the reach of a self-regulatory system is not necessarily limited by the extent of willing submission from those regulated; by virtue of their co-operative structure, self-regulatory systems can effectively control the activities even of individuals who have not made any voluntary gesture of submission. Moreover, while an individual's decision to subject himself to a system of self-regulation may be voluntarily taken, once taken, compliance with the rules imposed—at least by an effective system of self-regulation—ceases, for him, to be a matter of choice. Self-regulation is thus a concept distinct from self-discipline. The latter word may reasonably be used to describe the individual's attempts to control his own actions, but the former entails control by the individual's peers, subjection to whose judgment is central to the description of systems based upon it as regulatory. Self-discipline's only sanction is the individual conscience. The most characteristic sanction of self-regulation is exclusion, of varying kinds and to varying degrees, from participation in the activity regulated.

CRITICISMS OF SELF-REGULATION

Let me turn from defining self-regulation to a more detailed examination of the criticisms which are raised against it—or rather against its use for the regulation of commerce; clearly, many of these criticisms would be equally applicable to professional self-regulatory arrangements.

The most coherent statement of the objections that I have come across is in Ross Cranston's book *Consumers and the Law*.[3] Cranston's critique of self-regulation may be analysed under four heads. His first group of objections go to motivation. In his view "the motivation for business self-regulation is sometimes far removed from the sense of social responsibility which we are led to believe underlies it . . . there can be little doubt that much self-regulation has been influenced by fear of . . . more onerous governmental control." Secondly, he observes that "businesses have realised self-regulation can lead to positive commercial advantage." Thirdly, he identifies a "temptation for businesses to introduce self-regulation as a means of insulating themselves from competitive forces," to a point, indeed, where a given scheme, or one of its aspects, may be "void as an unreasonable constraint of trade."

Cranston's second group of objections concern what is, in his view, the inadequate implementation of self-regulation. There are four reasons for this on Cranston's analysis. First, "not all businesses . . . may adhere to the voluntary standards agreed on" and those who do not adhere "are usually the most likely to be employing disreputable practices." Secondly, voluntary standards are difficult to enforce because they are "mere window dressing . . . so general as to be relatively useless." Thirdly, "by the very nature of things, a trade association will be slow to enforce standards against its members . . . it will tend to allocate minimum forces to enforcement." And lastly, "It is too optimistic to think that a trade association, wholly supported by the subscriptions of its members and imbued with their values, will assume the same independent stance in implementing controls as a government agency."

Cranston's third group of objections is directed towards what he takes to be characteristic structural deficiencies in self-regulation. In the first place, it "can be weakened by the absence of a consumer voice in the formulation and implementation" of its controls, with the consequence that "voluntary standards are based more often than not on prevailing practices in industry"; in consequence, they "have a limited view of what is against the consumer interest" and may "not extend to the social consequences of advertising." Secondly, "almost invariably . . . self-regulation lacks independent machinery for its implementation and procedures which exist are likely to be shrouded in secrecy. Where independent representatives take part . . . they are typically in the minority and seem to be chosen for their pro-business or at least 'neutral' attitude."

Cranston's final objection is based on his suspicion that the introduction of plausible schemes of self-regulation acts to deter or postpone the introduction of legal controls. The only common criticism of self-regulation omitted from Cranston's catalogue is that which contrasts the sanctions available to it unfavourably with those avail-

---

[3] London (Weidenfeld and Nicholson) 1979.

able under law; and derives from the contrast the conclusion that there is nothing that can be attained by means of self-regulation that cannot be better and more certainly attained by law.

THE CRITICISMS CONSIDERED

One notices immediately the extent to which Cranston's critique is expressed in terms of qualified generalisations: likelihoods and possibilities rather than necessities or actualities. But no one doubts that in principle there *may* be bad self-regulatory systems—or even that good ones may from time to time fail to achieve what they set out to provide. There may be, after all—indeed there are—bad systems of law; ones motivated by desires other than that for justice; systems bad in content or bad in implementation. But that is not normally taken as justifying the wholesale dismissal of law as a tool of social control. The question we need to address first therefore is whether the weaknesses that Cranston says characterise self-regulation are either inherent or incapable of correction. At the outset we may note some of the positive aspects of the theory of self-regulation about which critics, if not entirely silent, are typically less than forthcoming.

THE POSITIVE CASE

Self-regulation in commerce rests upon the proposition that businessmen can (and do) share the majority of their fellow citizens' sense of responsibility to society at large. Self-regulation aims to mobilise this sentiment by creating a positive commitment among businessmen towards the effective implementation of regulations for which they are themselves responsible and in which they can take a legitimate pride. In this way self-regulation has the capacity to overcome one problem that confronts any non-consensual form of regulation, namely the tendency of those bound by it to do "the least the law requires and the most that it allows."

In addition, self-regulation through its practical orientation and its avoidance of unnecessary formality has inherent practical virtues, such as swiftness, flexibility, easy adaptation to changing circumstances and cheapness. It can set standards higher than those which a legislature may find it possible or desirable to prescribe. And the enforcement of these standards can be more commonsensical; less open to subversion by legalism.

Even on this basis, though, two central objections remain. Given the undeniable self-interest which creates and motivates self-regulation, is it not likely that its achievement must always be suspected of bias? And to the extent that it operates with at least tolerable efficiency and fairness, is there not a danger that it will disturb the optimum development of inherently superior legal controls?

MOTIVATION

The element of self-interest in the establishment of self-regulation is not, it appears to me, one that there is any attempt to disguise. Concealment is not merely impossible, it is unnecessary. There is no reason to suppose that the harnessing of self-interest to serve the broader purposes of society is undesirable *in principle*—even if we concede that the harness must be a good one if the horse is to remain under the rider's control. Self-regulation is a defining characteristic of the professional; it is thus a badge to be worn by the businessman with pride and not with shame. Nor is suspicion of external regulation necessarily irrational, or unhealthy. Recent British experience with the Bargain Offers Orders is in point here. The negative effects of over-regulation or ill-considered regulation can be felt not only by business but also by its customers. Inappropriate controls on advertising, whatever view one takes of its importance in economic terms, may lead to the loss or weakening of a useful, alternative, unofficial channel for the communication of information and opinion; and to an unnecessary reduction of marketing and hence of competitive effectiveness. Finally, of course, the mere fact that self-interest is known to underlie self-regulatory systems makes it less, not more, likely that it will have the effect of subverting the system or of leading it to operate in a way that goes against the public interest— which is why so much stress is placed in the ASA system for instance on publicity for the system and its actions.

The whole of this part of the case against self-regulation is in any case predicated on the assumption that the interests of trade and the consumer, because they are distinct, must necessarily be at odds. I cannot develop the point here, but it seems to me that it is far from obvious that this is so; indeed, it could be said that the case for the Directive is predicated on the assumption that they are in general the same.

A STUMBLING BLOCK FOR LEGISLATION?

But does self-regulation pre-empt government action? It is clear that no government is likely to be deterred from necessary legislation by the existence of *ineffective* alternatives to what it sets out to do; but if we suppose that self-regulation works well—and we have seen nothing so far to suggest that it cannot—must it be classed as undesirable because it constitutes a stumbling block in the way of legal regulation?

So far as the enforcement of existing legal rules is concerned, there would seem to be no need. (Cranston, for example, instances the British courts' striking-down of an attempt to use self-regulatory methods in a way which would have had the effect of preventing competition among retail chemists; and parallels for this action can be found world-wide.)

We may accept however that, if self-regulation is seen as dealing well with a given problem, the probability of new, legally based, controls to deal with the same problem is thereby reduced. The question whether that outcome is disadvantageous to consumers brings out an unstated assumption that often underlies criticism. This is that law and self-regulation are in some sense mutually exclusive concepts; with the result that the initiation and development of any self-regulatory system necessarily poses a challenge to the supremacy of law, a challenge which becomes more serious to the extent that the system succeeds.

LAW AND SELF-REGULATION

Can two normative systems be mutually exclusive unless both claim supremacy and dispute an identical field of operation? And is that the position in any of the countries which have developed self-regulatory systems? Certainly there is no such struggle for supremacy in Britain as far as advertising is concerned. Sir Gordon Borrie's introduction to the most recent annual report on the Office of Fair Trading recognises the appropriateness in British circumstances of relying on different "horses" for different "courses." More generally, it is a cardinal principle of all systems based on the International Chamber of Commerce's advertising code that the law shall take precedence.

Concern over the relationship of law and self-regulation also arises in two other ways. It is sometimes suggested (rather than argued) that the constitutional supremacy of law entails its practical omnicompetence; alternatively it may be said that advertising is too limited a field for the operation of two distinct forms of control. Neither of these propositions seems to me to hold water. The law no less than its alternatives has limits to its effectiveness; and experience has shown that it is precisely in those areas where law is at its weakest that self-regulation is at its strongest.

THE LIMITS OF LAW

I do not need to dwell upon the legislative and enforcement restraints which in many areas must limit the availability of law as a tool of social control; suffice it to remark that there are inherent practical limits under our constitution—and I would suppose most others—to the numbers of new laws which can be created or of old laws which can be amended or repealed. There are political limits to the extent to which delegated legislation can be applied. There are problems, too, in the formulation of controls which may be exacerbated by the British tradition of legislative drafting (which may prove particularly acute where much must depend, as it does in advertising, upon subjective judgments as to meaning and speculation as to the effects of the activity controlled).

Then there are the problems of implementation. The omnipotence of the legislature only entails the omnicompetence of its agents in a peculiarly simple-minded constitutional theory. Even where the state has responsiblity for enforcement, the funds available for discharging that responsibility are finite. The importance of the ready availability of funds is of course apparent where rights must be asserted in the courts by the individual trader or consumer—or by bodies acting in their name.

HOW EFFECTIVE IS THE LAW?

Do these stringencies mean that the effectiveness of legal controls is seriously impaired? So far as advertising is concerned, the answer to that question must depend largely upon one's assessment of the scale of the problem posed by that part of it which is misleading or unfair; I shall return to this issue a little later when considering the effectiveness of the British self-regulatory system. Suffice it to note here that this is an area where, on the one hand, the nature of the practice which is being controlled is so multifarious (there are said to be in Great Britain alone as many as 25,000,000 different advertisements published each year and the numbers of individual trading transactions must run into thousands of millions) and where, on the other hand, the nature of the individual offence is often trivial.

In Britain, in contrast to the position in several of its European partners, consumer protection has developed as an essentially public responsibility, with enforcement lying in the hands of local authorities whose trading standards officers have a wide range of responsibilities of which the control of advertisement content is only one. It is interesting that, although most of the legislation for which trading standards officers are responsible is backed by criminal sanctions, very few prosecutions in fact are brought in relation to the volume of trade, and of these very few relate to matters of advertisement content. Where advertising does form the subject matter of a prosecution, it is most likely because of the advertiser's failure to observe one or other of the direct requirements for disclosure, such as trader status, rather than because of attempts to mislead in more devious ways. The reasons for the low number of prosecutions overall have been examined by Lidstone and his colleagues.[4] Their conclusion is that, not surprisingly, trading standards officers regard much of the legislation they have the responsibility of enforcing as primarily educative and preventative in character. The principal function of the officer thus becomes one of encouraging compliance by means of advice, warnings and informal conciliation, with prosecutions being resorted to only after all else has failed. This attitude is if anything reinforced by the fact that most infractions of consumer protection legislation are offences of strict liability. It may be, as ECLG hints, that a change to David Tench's preferred "middle system" of administrative law might change this situation; but it has to be said

[4] Research Study No. 10 for the Royal Commission on Criminal Procedure (H.M.S.O.).

there is no sign at present of the British government being prepared to make that experiment.

Attempts have been made, of course, through the Office of Fair Trading in this country and through bodies elsewhere such as the Federal Trade Commission in the United States, to overcome the disproportion between the numbers of matters pursued by the official machinery and the numbers of transactions proceeding, by the publication of officially sponsored codes or officially authorised rules providing guidance of a more or less compulsive nature to those operating in a particular sector of the market.

This topic cannot be pursued here, but for our present purposes I would underline that whenever a statutory body chooses to play a persuasive rather than a compulsive role, one of the most often touted strengths of the law, namely the severity of its sanctions in comparison with those of self-regulation, is to that extent compromised.

THE STRENGTHS OF LEGAL CONTROL

This is not to claim that legal control does not have its unique advantage—ultimate compulsive power; the nature of the sanctions which it wields; its appropriateness where issues with major constitutional effects are involved; even its theoretically unlimited scope. There are, equally clearly, areas where it would be inappropriate for influence to be wielded except through the democratic process, and hence by using legal means. (The question whether cigarette advertising—or the advertising of any other freely sold product—should be forbidden seems to me to be self-evidently such an issue.) The advantages of legal control are real advantages and it is no part of the case for self-regulation to suggest that they can be equalled, at all points. It is however clear that legal, no less than extra-legal, systems have weaknesses as well as strengths. It is for this reason that there exists scope for the complementary activity of self-regulation.

HOW EFFECTIVE IS SELF-REGULATION?

I turn now to criticisms which imply that self-regulation is inadequately implemented and/or structurally deficient. Given that self-regulation is a legitimate activity, in other words, is it either as effective as it should be or as fair as it ought to be?

Before considering the essentially positive answers to these questions given by the Office of Fair Trading and the Department of Trade Working Party it may be helpful briefly to consider the structure of the present advertising self-regulatory system in Britain. This has been described as a tripartite, two tier system: tripartite because the industry body, the Code of Advertising Practice Committee, has in membership trade associations representative of all sides of the advertising business—advertiser, advertising agencies and most importantly media; two-tier because the whole of the CAP

Committee's work, including the drafting of the Code, is subject to the oversight of an independent body, the Advertising Standards Authority. The individual members of CAP organisations are each bound as a condition of membership to support the self-regulatory system. In this way, the direct scope of the system is such as to account for the overwhelming majority of advertisements within its area (*i.e.* excluding television and radio as controlled by the IBA). Overwhelming because, although it is only major advertisers who are in membership of the advertising association, and major agencies in the agency association, the great bulk of advertisements produced by those outside must still pass through media. And the media associations, now including the Association of Free Newspapers, account for all except a handful of the advertisements to which the public is exposed. There *are* advertisements which are created and published outside this system, but they are few, and what evidence there is suggests that they are no more likely to offend the Code than those produced within the system. In any event, breaches of the Code are not, in my experience, for the most part the consequence of intentional dishonesty. Rather they arise from carelessness or ignorance; and my experience has also been that those who are ignorant of what the Code requires are generally very ready to conform to it when made aware of their obligations.

Given that the scope of the ASA/CAP system is as extensive as it is, what truth is there in the suggestion that the rules themselves—the two Codes: the British Code of Advertising Practice and the British Code of Sales Promotion Practice—are too vague in their requirements or not stringent enough?

In truth, the content of rules is scarcely an issue in the real world. Most argument is not about what should be done, but about who should do it. Nonetheless, it is the case that the standards which the Codes lay down undeniably often exceed in strictness those prescribed by the law (indeed it is their purpose to do so). And their drafting is regularly reconsidered and improved in clarity, with a wholly fresh edition of each appearing every five years or so and containing not just updated rules, but also new rules devised to deal with novel situations. Consultations are undertaken before publication of these regular revisions with the Office of Fair Trading, the Consumers' Association, the National Consumer Council and other external bodies. I have no reason to believe that any of them finds the Code seriously wanting, even if there are minor points on which each of them would choose to act differently.

But what about sanctions? As we have seen, this is one area in which the law indubitably has the edge if severity or compulsion are to be the tests. But it is not the aim of self-regulation to supplant law; it aims, as I have said, to complement it—in the area of sanctions as elsewhere. Advertising self-regulation acts predominantly by preventing the publication or repetition of misleading advertisements—this it can do as quickly as the technology involved in publication will allow. The interception of offending advertising—as opposed to the sanctioning of the offender—is not something which is easily achieved under British law as it presently exists. And even if an injunctive remedy is introduced after reception of the Directive, it will not be widely available. On the other hand, it is the central means self-regulation has of securing compliance, which is why it is so important that media should be fully behind the Code.

Given the low rates of prosecution we have seen, the adverse publicity given to breaches of the Code by the circulation to media of the ASA's regular monthly case report (and within the industry of the CAP equivalent) is also useful, not only as a sanction, but as a warning to the public. These reports also, incidentally, give the lie to Cranston's claim that self-regulatory activities are typically shrouded in secrecy.

That the system's means of securing compliance are effective for its purpose would be of little value if they were not impartially applied. Can one expect a self-regulatory system to be stern enough with its erring brethren? The danger that lies in too closed a system was perceived at the outset, and since 1962—one year after the system was set up—the Advertising Standards Authority, composed as it is of a majority of persons with no financial or professional interest in advertising, has been the final authority not merely on the content of the Code but on its implementation. The governing Council of the Authority is small and its members sit as individuals. Successive Chairmen of the Authority have taken great care nonetheless to see that, within the limits on size imposed by the overriding need to enable decisions to be taken firmly and swiftly, the Council reflects as well as possible the diversity of national life.

In short, the dangers of undemanding standards, affecting too few to be of relevance, and slackly enforced by institutions too well disposed to the advertising business, were seen from the outset as essential to be avoided. To the extent that criticisms of self-regulation are based on the assumption that these dangers are characteristic of the ASA/CAP system, they are, I believe, misconceived.

THE O.F.T. AND DEPARTMENT OF TRADE REVIEWS OF SELF-REGULATION

The ASA/CAP system assumed its present form in 1974, when arrangements were made for it to be funded on a more generous scale by the advertising business than had previously been the case. Since then it has been the subject of two external examinations. The first, in 1978, was by the Office of Fair Trading; the second, in 1980, by a working party of the Department of Trade.

The Director-General of Fair Trading summed up the outcome of his office's scrutiny of the system by saying that it was "working well." He made a number of detailed suggestions for improved procedures, the majority of which have since been implemented (the other suggestions having been, by agreement, withdrawn). The

Director-General added that he could "see no justification for drastic new legislative controls" to supplant what self-regulation was doing; were such new controls necessary, "it would reflect more on those who enforce existing legislation than on those who administered the self-regulatory system"—a point of particular relevance when we come in a moment to consider the scale of the problem which confronts regulators of all kinds. Instead of a new legislative order, Sir Gordon proposed a better integration of self-regulatory and statutory controls, with a power being developed which would enable him to use the courts to provide a direct back-up to self-regulation. This proposal was welcomed both by the ASA and by the advertising business; subsequently it was endorsed by the Department of Trade Working Party. It reflected earlier proposals which had been put forward by the National Consumer Council. It has not been implemented, pending resolution of the long debate over the Advertising Directive.

The Office of Fair Trading's review of the operation of self-regulation was based upon a national sample survey of press advertisements. The survey showed that 93 per cent. of the advertisements examined conformed to the British Code of Advertising Practice. Although in most assessments a "pass" rate of 93 per cent. might be thought highly creditable, it was remarked that with around 25,000,000 advertisments appearing each year a 7 per cent failure rate entailed no less than 1,750,000 advertisements per annum offending the Code. Even though some of the assessments, upon which the O.F.T.'s survey calculations were based, subsequently proved to be ill-founded and despite the fact that, of the advertisements which "failed," few did so, in the view of the O.F.T. assessors, because they were greatly deceptive, the fact remains that figures of this size suggest a continuing problem of substantial proportions. And so we need to know how this accords with what we know from other sources of the scale of the problem before we can assess the effectiveness of a system which, centrally, deals with only about 30,000 advertisements each year.

THE SCALE OF THE PROBLEM

The first survey in which, as far as I am aware, a serious attempt was made to assess the extent to which advertisements offended against acceptable standards was conducted by the European Bureau of Consumer Unions (BEUC) in 1972. This found that 14 per cent of the British sample of advertisements examined were open to objection, but the survey is of interest primarily because of its purported finding that advertisements in the Federal Republic of Germany were about five times more likely to mislead consumers than those which were published in the United Kingdom. Even if one takes these figures as indicative only, this result does seem to cast doubt on the argument (sometimes put forward in support of the Directive) that an essential element in any system of legislative control must be the ascription of rights to associations, individuals, competitors and so on, as a replacement for, or alternative to, control by public officials.

Another source of information about the scale of the problem is opinion surveys. A Community Survey in 1976 showed a total of 78 per cent of those questioned in the United Kingdom agreeing with the statement "Advertising often misleads consumers." A survey conducted at the same time also in the United Kingdom by the Advertising Association asked a similar question, but put in less abstract terms: respondents were asked whether they agreed that "The advertisements you see are often misleading." 67 per cent. said they did agree. At the same time, the same respondents were asked whether they agreed that *they* were "frequently misled by the advertisements" they saw. To this only 28 per cent. of respondents were ready to reply affirmatively.

A similarly contradictory picture was revealed when the questions were about the ability of advertising to make people buy things they did not want. The European Community survey got 78 per cent. agreement with the proposition that "advertising often makes consumers buy goods they do not really need" (which is perhaps less than wholly surprising, given the relatively restricted range of products than can be described as necessities). The Advertising Association survey got a lower positive response (50 per cent.) to the same question expressed in terms of wants rather than needs; in part, no doubt, because it is hard to see how a purchase can be made without there in fact being a "want," however evanescent, involved. When the proposition was personalised, and the respondents were asked whether they agreed that "Advertising makes *me* buy things I do not want" (author's italics), the proportion agreeing fell to 15 per cent.

One problem with such research is that it forces people to have views—pro or anti—about a subject which other surveys show they regard as of little general importance. (Only 2 per cent. of an Advertising Association sample in 1980 regarded advertising as a matter requiring "immediate attention or change.") The effect of this artificial forcing of the issue may be exacerbated by the phrasing of the questions themselves. It would be interesting to see what the result would be if the questions suggested "Advertising doesn't often mislead people," "Advertising doesn't make me buy things I don't want," etc.

Given the surveys in the form that we have them, one follow up exercise is interesting in that it sought to discover what, if anything, in the real world corresponds to the generalised objections which are expressed about advertisements. The AA 1980/1981 survey asked a sample of those who had evinced hostile attitudes to advertising in general to monitor the advertisements they saw over one month. This exercise produced only a handful of advertisements to which objections were more than expressions of personal distaste.

This result thus accorded more closely with the O.F.T. survey's indication of the percentage of offensive advertisements than with assertions by the respondents when asked unspecific questions. Further evidence of what it is that consumers are in fact objecting to, when they express dislike of advertising in general, in terms of it being misleading, comes from a survey conducted in six European Countries in 1978 by Campbell-Ewald International, an advertising agency. The central finding of this survey was summed up as "Advertising bores people"—and it is clear enough that if people are repeatedly exposed to material they find boring, their attitude to it is not likely to be positive—a supposition which is underlined by the survey's findings that most people see most advertisements as, in essence, similar. If this is indeed the case, it offers one explanation of how the minority of unacceptable advertisements come to be regarded as typical of advertising as a whole. And this, in turn, goes some way to reconciling the four-fifths of the population who appear, in some surveys, to think that advertising is misleading, with the tiny percentage who in the United Kingdom complain about it, whether to the statutory authorities or to the self-regulatory system, or were able to find misleading advertisements in the AA 1981 follow-up.

The Advertising Standards Authority conducts biennial surveys of public awareness of its role and functions. The most recent research, in 1982, showed that 23 per cent. of the population of the United Kingdom aged over 16 were aware, without being prompted, of the ASA's existence. From this 10,000,000 or so people came no more than 8,000 complaints in 1982, of which only 13 per cent. proved on investigation to be well-founded. Nor do our files show that this is because there is some kind of advertisement about which people are reluctant to complain. Although O.F.T. figures are not analysable in this way, an examination of the Annual Reports of Trading Standards Authorities suggests that complaints to statutory authorities about advertisements also run at a low level. There is, in fact, an extraordinary disproportion between the number of advertisements which are complained about and the millions of unacceptable ones which must exist if surveys of this problem are to be believed.

Part of the problem is no doubt semantic. None of the surveys discussed above, with the exception of the AA 1980/81 follow-up, has ever attempted to ascertain what view it is that respondents are expressing when they agree that advertisements are misleading. Those who interpret these figures as showing the ineffectiveness of self-regulation assume that these answers relate to an attribute of advertisements which ought to lead to their being prevented or removed by self-regulatory action (though in truth the reflection, as we saw the O.F.T. survey recognised, should be upon "those who enforce existing legislation"). But it is at least conceivable that "misleading" reflects the respondents' perception that advertisements, of their very nature, are partial, persuasive communications, neither offered nor to be understood as neutral or complete. That they are neither, may be viewed as sufficient reason for criticism; it is not however a demonstration that, objectively, the advertisements concerned have the capacity to mislead in the sense that concerns regulators. Nor can we say that the evidence entitles us to conclude that the scale of the problem is such as to show either that self-regulation is ineffective, or that it can only deal with an insignificant proportion of what there is.

IS SELF-REGULATION FAIR?

There remains the issue of fairness to be addressed. Just as important as the consumer interest in the implementation of a self-regulatory system is the interest of the practitioner in ensuring that he receives fair treatment. There is an evident danger in any system of self-regulation that it may be used oppressively—and the argument is sometimes raised that any system in which the prospective (or even actual) competitors of the advertiser may sit in judgment upon him cannot be acceptable. To the extent that the advertiser who is the subject of a complaint has voluntarily submitted himself to the system, the argument carries little weight. It is of the very nature of self-regulation that judgment should be by one's peers. But as we have seen, one part of the effectiveness of self-regulation rests on its ability, through the co-operation of the media, to extend its sanctions even to those who have not given assent.

In any event it would not be acceptable to ignore the rules of natural justice. One central function of the Advertising Standards Authority is precisely to ensure that the system's decisions about the acceptability of advertisements are not based upon *ex parte* allegations or considerations external to the Code, that they are subject to independent scrutiny, and that they are publicly recorded.

It is, however, important to understand the differences between self-regulatory procedures and those of legal enforcement systems. These are inclined to be obscured by the use in both areas, for reasons of convenience so far as self-regulation is concerned, of words such as "case," "offender," "adjudication" and so on. Self-regulation works not by offering a do-it-yourself parallel to law—a contest in which it would come off an inevitable second best—but by drawing on a concept of common commitment which is absent from law enforcement (in practice, if not in constitutional theory). The characteristic adversarial element in law enforcement is replaced in self-regulation by co-operation. The function of a body such as ASA is not to adjudicate as would a court between advertiser and complainant, but to state, upon the application of either, what the Code, and hence the public interest, requires in the particular set of circumstances drawn to its attention. Those who support the self-regulatory system accept such a statement as binding upon them and adjust their actions and policies accordingly. An advertiser is not put under compulsion to do this or to withhold from doing that. He either accepts that, by virtue of his freely-given commitment, he should adjust his advertisement or, if unwilling to make the commitment himself, faces the practical impossibility of being able to place the advertisement elsewhere because of the commitment of those with whom he seeks to contract. Voluntary adherence by media to a common set of standards cannot be represented as an actionable restraint of trade, since none of the individuals who make up the aggregate is, in fact or in law, under any obligation to contract except upon such basis as he chooses—though that basis once chosen must be applied equally to all if competition is not to be actionably hindered. The Code and the system for enforcing it have of course to be registered as a restrictive practice, but it should be noted that the Director General of Fair Trading has indicated to the Secretary of State that the restrictions contained in the advertising self-regulatory system are not of such significance as to warrant investigation by the court and it is understood that his reason for so doing derives from his conviction that overall the system operates so as to benefit the consumer.

THE POLITICAL ACCEPTABILITY OF SELF-REGULATION

Self-regulation, as I have described it, is a fair and effective complement to legal modes of control. In conclusion, I would like to say a word about its political acceptability.

Self-regulatory systems in advertising control are now widespread around the world. Few of the developed nations of the West do not have such an alternative to their national legal arrangements. Codes of Practice developed within the business have been published for advertising in socialist countries such as Hungary, Yugoslavia and the People's Republic of China. Against this background, it is scarcely necessary to labour the point of the general acceptability in some areas of self-regulation, though it may be added that governments of various political colours have gone beyond mere toleration and have expressed gratitude for the contibution made by self-regulation to advertising control.

If, however, one takes political acceptability as connoting general acceptance of the politically active classes within society, the picture is different. On the one hand, many socialists see self-regulation as tarred with the same brush as advertising itself—an objectionable by-product of the capitalist system. On the other hand, one meets opposition from some consumer activists whose motivation is not necessarily socialist in orientation, or indeed political in a party sense at all.

I suspect that the problem arises in part from a feeling of exclusion from being allowed or encouraged to make any contribution to self-regulation. If this is so, then the fault may well lie with those responsible for self-regulation for being unwilling to enter into dialogue. On the other hand, consumer professionals sometimes seem not to grasp the considerable reservations which exist—not just among businessmen—about proposals, such as those in the Directive, which may involve according *locus standi* to groups which are not necessarily—or even commonly—representative in character, so that they can pursue the presumed interests of those who are thus "represented."

One accepts that problems exist which the "class action" approach is intended to overcome; but it is equally clear that unless the exercise of any such right of audience is subject to effective limitation (which, one suspects, reduces much of its appeal for those who advocate it) a danger exists of the courts becoming a mere annexe to the political arena.

Whether the situation is generally so serious as to make it desirable to run this risk I will not pretend to know enough to say; but in advertising, the risk, on the basis of the evidence we have studied, would seem to be greater than any benefit which might accrue. That there is a valuable role for organised consumers no longer needs to be demonstrated, in the light of the achievements of bodies such as our own Consumers' Association. It remains open to question whether their reputation would be enhanced by bodies claiming a similar constituency becoming regular participants in litigation—even though their motives were as pure as Ross Cranston might wish.

V

Marketing Practices

Ludwig Kraemer[1]

As the EEC does not have general competence, as a nation-state, but derives its competence to act from the EEC Treaty, any measure which is undertaken at Community level needs a specific justification. This is true in particular of matters which affect consumers' interests, because the EEC Treaty does not expressly mention consumer policy or consumer protection.

Therefore it seems appropriate to discuss first the question of Community competence for the protection of economic interests of consumers, particularly as this competence continues to be contested. We also have to bear in mind that legal arguments for or against such a Community competence are very often influenced by other factors, especially by vested interests, power and national sovereignty.

ARGUMENTS FOR COMMUNITY COMPETENCE

The following arguments can be advanced in favour of a Community competence in matters of marketing practices or of protection of economic interests of consumers in general.

1. Article 36 gives, for those areas expressly mentioned in that Article and especially for the protection of health and safety of persons, only a residual competence to member countries.[2] Member States may deal with issues enumerated in that article, but only as long as and to the extent that there is no Community legislation. It would appear that if the Community, even in those most important areas, is competent to issue rules in addition to the Member States, the Community should all the more be competent to issue rules for economic aspects which are not expressly enumerated in that article.

2. Rules for marketing, sales promotion, advertising or commercial practices, which differ from country to country, require the producer or trader to adapt his distribution methods to those differing rules. They therefore prevent him from planning and realising marketing strategies inside the Common Market, which are independent

---

[1] See p.25. The views expressed in this paper are those of the author and are not to be attributed to the Commission of the European Communities
[2] This is confirmed by several decisions of the Court of Justice of the EEC and seems to be generally accepted.

of national frontiers. This was expressly recognised by the European Court of Justice in Case 152/78 (advertising), Case 58/80 (*Dansk Supermarked*) and Case 286/81 (*Oosthoek*).[3] The Court admitted that national rules concerning the marketing of goods restricted the free circulation of products in the EEC and constituted therefore a "measure having equivalent effect" forbidden under Article 30 of the Treaty. However, the Court found that such rules could be justified if they were necessary to protect consumers.

But it seems logical to conclude that where national rules, adopted in the economic interest of consumers, may restrict the free circulation of goods inside the EEC, the EEC is competent to legislate by virtue of Article 100, because these restrictions directly influence the establishment and the functioning of the Common Market. It is indeed inconceivable that national rules may legitimately restrict inter-Community trade without the Community being entitled to eliminate these restrictions by the approximation of laws. Thus whenever a national rule of protection of economic interests of consumers is justified despite Article 30, the Community is competent to proceed under Article 100.

3. The costs of marketing and sale promotion account for a considerable part of the production and distribution costs.[4] Rules in favour of consumers in these areas therefore have a considerable impact on prices of goods and services. The Select Committee considered these effects as not being "direct" in the sense of Article 100.[5] However, in Case 91/79 (detergents) the Court of Justice of the EEC mentioned that rules for the protection of health or the environment justified charges by companies affected by them; without an approximation of national laws competition could thus be substantially distorted.[6] This statement can be directly used for rules protecting the economic interests of consumers, as such rules are equally cost-relevant.

4. Advertisements and, gradually, sales promotions cross national boundaries more and more. Trade and industry organise themselves more and more at international or European level. Under these circumstances the establishment of a Common Market requires that rules on the misleading nature of advertisements or on marketing practices should not differ significantly from one region of the EEC to the other. In a Common Market, where manufacturing and marketing standards for goods and services are more and more harmonised, it does not make much sense to countenance considerable

---

[3] Case 152/78 *Commission* v. *France* [1980] E.C.R. 2299, (alcohol); Case 58/80 *Dansk Supermarked* v. *Imerco* [1981] E.C.R. 181; Case 286/81 *Openbaar Ministerie* v. *Oosthoek's Uitgevers-Maatschappij BV* [1982] E.C.R. 4575.
[4] To give an example: the British Price Commission found, for pharmaceutical advertising, that "for a number of well-established products advertising expenditure is as much as 25 per cent. of sales revenue" (Report of May 17th, 1978, point 9.2)
[5] Select Committee, *Approximation of legislations* . . . London, 1978.
[6] Case 91/79 *Commission* v. *Italy* [1980] E.C.R. 1099.

differences in the protection of the consumers against misleading advertising or undesirable marketing practices. Such differences are, in the long run, incompatible with an harmonious development of economics and a balanced raising of economics (Article 2).

5. All the above arguments can be summarised in the statement that an Economic Community, which has the task of establishing a Common Market and of making it function, must have the competence to approximate national rules which aim at protecting economic interests of citizens of this Economic Community, which differ and which restrict trade within the Community.

These comments on Community competence do not suggest that Article 100 or 235 of the Treaty oblige the Community to elaborate immediately rules about the protection of economic interests of consumers. Both articles give an extremely wide discretion to the Community legislators to take action or not. Both articles require unanimous decisions of the Council. This will induce the Commission to submit only such proposals to the Council that have a fair chance of being adopted within a reasonable time. Legal considerations are at least sometimes superseded by questions of political opportunity.

PREMIUM OFFERS

This can well be illustrated by the subject of premium offers. Under the preliminary programme of the EEC,[7] which was adopted by the unanimous Council of Ministers after 18 months of word-by-word discussion, the protection of economic interests of consumers was to be assured "by legislative measures," which were "either to be harmonised at Community level or directly taken at this level" (point 18). As a priority action, the Commission was to submit to the Council proposals for appropriate action on premium offers (point 25). The Commission then ordered a study on the subject matter, which was never published but which became known in some member countries. The reaction to that study caused the Commission to announce that any Community action on premium offers was not necessary,[8] a statement which the Council deleted from the second consumer programme. In 1982 the Court of Justice ruled that the Dutch Act on premium offers was compatible with Article 30, though it restricted trade within the Community.[9]

Is the one complaint against the Dutch Act sufficient to justify or even to require EEC action? Nobody knows how many companies are likewise affected by the absence of EEC-wide rules. Any attempt at measuring the intensity of any such effect would also have to consider eventual future profits.

[7] O.J. 1975 C 92/1.
[8] Proposal for a second consumer programme, O.J. 1980 C 218/3, point 30.
[9] Case 286/81 Openbaar Ministerie [1982] E.C.R. 4575.

These considerations indicate that it is a question rather of political discretion than of legal competence whether the Community will legislate on premium offers. There is no indication that under the present economic and political climate any such rules will be proposed in the near future. Neither is there any pressure from the side of consumer organisations, nor from traders, nor from the European Parliament.

ADVERTISING

This paper will not deal with questions of misleading and unfair advertising, as there is another paper concentrating on that subject.[10] Community action in other areas of advertising has been very modest. The EEC directive on the labelling of food[11] applies also to the advertising of food. The Commission has, in pursuance of that Directive, submitted a proposal for a Directive on food claims that are to be forbidden or restricted[12]; these claims deal mainly with health questions. The proposal met strong criticism from the European Parliament, which considered it to be unnecessary and objected also to the approach adopted by the Commission.[13] It is therefore not yet certain whether the proposal will be adopted in the near future.

Regulation 355/79 contains general rules on advertising for wine which forbid any misleading advertising.[14] However, there are no general rules limiting alcohol advertising. The European federation of alcoholic drink producers in 1980 formulated a code of conduct on alcohol advertising, but wihout any monitoring machinery. The question of common rules for alcohol advertising may reach a solution once we enter the satellite television era, as some member countries allow for such advertising on the television. There are no concrete plans at present to create common standards for protecting consumers' interests against these forms of advertising.

As regards tobacco advertising the Commission announced in 1978 that a Directive would be prepared.[15] Since then all such plans have been frozen and are not being actively pursued.

In the area of pharmaceutical advertising the Commission submitted as long ago as 1967 a proposal for a Directive, which was later withdrawn.[16] The Commission announced a new proposal in 1977 and even tried to prevent some member countries from adopt-

---

[10] See S. Freedman, *ante*, p.39.
[11] Dir. 79/112; O.J. 1979 L 33/1.
[12] O.J. 1981 C 198/4.
[13] EP, O.J. 1983 C 96/93; the Economic and Social Committee largely agreed, O.J. 1981 C 343/19.
[14] O.J. 1979 L 54/99, in particular Article 43.
[15] See Debates of the European Parliament, January 17, 1978, p. 91 (Mr. Burke); see also written question 798/78, O.J. 1979 C 45/27.
[16] O.J. 1967 248/18.

ing national rules.[17] In 1980, however, the Commission abandoned its attempts,[18] which did not stop the Council deciding in 1981 that pharmaceutical advertising rules should soon be adopted.[19] It does not seem likely that a Directive will be elaborated in the near future.

The pharmaceutical industry adopted in 1971 a European code of principles for advertising for pharmaceuticals which was revised in 1982. It might well be that this code will gain importance, once new technologies (satellite television, cable television) have gained importance inside the EEC.

The Commission is not preparing any propsals in the area of sales promotion and it is unlikely to do so within the next few years.

DOORSTEP CONTRACTS—"COOLING-OFF"

In the area of marketing practices the proposal for a Directive on contracts which are negotiated away from business premises should be mentioned. This proposal was made in 1977 and amended in 1978.[20] Since then it has been under discussion within the Council and, though most of the legal problems have been solved in one way or the other, it is not at all clear whether the Directive will ever be adopted.

The proposal of the Commission had essentially three aims:

(1) the introduction of a seven day cooling-off period for all contracts made away from business premises, which would allow the consumer to cancel the contract within that time;
(2) a written form for contracts made away from business premises;
(3) complementary rules in order to avoid the cooling-off period being excluded or shortened.

The Directive was to be of general application, as the philosophy behind it was independent of any specific type of contract: the cooling-off period and the written form were suggested because the consumer, when negotiating a contract away from business premises, was normally not prepared for contractual negotiations and thus was taken by surprise. Furthermore he had had no opportunity of comparing the offer with similar offers.

During the discussions within the Council, however, it became obvious that a general written form of doorstep contracts had no chance of being unanimously accepted. Similarly a number of contracts were to be excluded from the scope of application of the Directive, in particular insurance contracts, agency mail order contracts and contracts on shares and stocks. Even with these amend-

---

[17] See written question 777/78, O.J. 1979 C 33/7.
[18] See written question 563/81, O.J. 1981 C 295/7.
[19] Second consumer programme, O.J. 1981 C 133/1, point 19.
[20] O.J. 1977 C 22/6; amended O.J. 1978 C 127/6.

ments objections on different basic points of the proposal are still being pursued.

UNFAIR CONTRACT TERMS

Unfair contract terms are mentioned in both EEC consumer programmes. Indeed, one must realise that services are increasingly being distributed on the same contract terms. Whether a Fiat is bought in France or in Denmark, or a Philips refrigerator in the United Kingdom or in the Netherlands, the contract terms which accompany the product are essentially the same. Up to now there has been little research on this subject, but it is a fact that the same contract clause is applied by the same company in different legal systems. The philosophy of a Common Market can hardly accept that such a clause—for instance a clause which allows a unilateral amendment of the contract price—is considered unfair in one part of the EEC but not in another.

The Commission started work on unfair contract terms in 1976, but stopped in 1977 after having produced a preliminary draft.[21] In 1979 a green paper on unfair contract terms was announced, but it has not yet been published.[22] The reasons for this slow progress lie in the fact that France, the United Kingdom and Germany adopted some legislation between 1976 and 1978, while Denmark has had legislation since 1974. In the Netherlands, Belgium and Luxemburg, bills were being prepared and are still under consideration. Thus one might well argue that the time has passed for the Community legislators to intervene.

Other difficulties add to this inconvenience. It looks as if any rule of unfair contract terms will have to be accompanied by a flexible control mechanism, which would be able to supervise permanently the use which is made of general contract terms, to get unfair clauses eliminated and to impose sanctions on abuses.

Member States seem hardly ready to accept any such proposal from the Commission. The arguments are all well known: the national system functions all right; there are only a few complaints about unfair contract terms; control machinery would be too expensive; it would be up to national authorities to decide upon any such control machinery.

It is therefore unlikely that any Community action will tackle the problem of unfair contract terms in a horizontal way. Rather it seems likely that specific areas will be tackled, such as package holidays, air transport, car purchases, etc.

---

[21] Doc. SEPC/384/76—The document is published by Alpa-Bassone, *Il consumatore e l'Europa*, Padua, 1979.
[22] Proposal for a second consumer programme, O.J. 1980 C 218/3, point 30. (Since this paper was given the green paper has been published.)

CONCLUSION

When we summarise the Community activity in the area of sale promotion and marketing practices, we note little progress. This situation reflects the difficulties in which the Community finds itself generally, quite independently of consumer policy issues. Consumer policy issues form part of policy issues and, as "Europe" is not going strong, it is no wonder that rules aiming at a protection of the market citizen encounter so many difficulties.

VI

Free Movement of Goods and Consumer Protection

The Implications for National and European Consumer Law of the Case Law of the E.C. Court of Justice Since the "Cassis de Dijon" Decision.

Jules Stuyck[1]

PART 1: THE EEC TREATY, MARKET INTEGRATION AND THE CONSUMER

Article 2 of the EEC. Treaty reads: "The Community shall have as its task, by establishing a common market and progressively approximating the economic policies of Member States, to promote throughout the Community a harmonious development of economic activities, a continuous and balanced expansion, an increase in stability, an accelerated raising of the standard of living and closer relations between the States belonging to it." One will notice that the establishment of a common market—to be discussed further—is not an end in itself, but an instrument to achieve a certain number of goals of which one is the raising of the standard of living. This (sometimes illusory) objective only refers to one aspect of the consumer interest and is dependent on the distribution and consumption function[2] but nevertheless it follows clearly from Article 2 that the establishment of a common market must take place with regard being paid to the economic interest of the European consumer.

At the same time it follows clearly from Article 2 that the ultimate EEC. objectives, amongst which is the raising of the standard of living, have to be pursued by way of a common market and an approximation of the economic policies of the Member States. These two means are in fact the ends of practical community policy.

The "common market" concept is fairly problematic. The EEC

---

[1] University of Leuven, Belgium; Member of the Brussels Bar.
[2] Bourgoignie, Th., "European Community Consumer Law: Actual Achievements and Potentials for the Future," *European Consumer Law*, Louvain-la-Neuve, 1982, p. 36; expressly the consumer is only named in two Articles of the Treaty: Article 39 (agricultural policy) and Article 85(3) (competition): Krämer, L., "Uniform Legislation in diverse Legal Cultures: Experiences from the E.E.C. Harmonization Process," *European Consumer Law*, p. 156.

Treaty does not lead and has not led to a common market. Community law has become little more—to take the words of Jacques Pelkmans—than a "custom union plus."[3] Only in three areas (transport, agriculture, trade policy) does the Treaty confer the necessary powers on the community institutions in order to achieve a real market integration. A common market without at least a certain degree of approximation, or at the very least co-ordination, of economic policy and (thus) of legislation seems illusory. The discussion on disparities in car prices between Member States[4] is a good example. The two means, the Common Market and approximation of the economic policies, are distinct but closely linked.[5]

The establishment of a common market is directly and negatively affected by still existing disparities in technical and other standards and legislation. The economic crisis has increased the tendency of national protectionism.

Consumer protection in the EEC can be related to economic, social and political integration.[6] The major objective, as appears from Article 2, is economic integration: "For the purposes of Article 2, the activities of the Community, thus Article 3, shall include, . . . a) the elimination, as between Member States, of customs duties and of quantitative restrictions on the import and export of goods, and of all other measures having equivalent effect . . . ." The free movement of goods (Articles 30 *et seq.*) is clearly one of the most important instruments for achieving the Common Market objective. The same can be said of "the institution of a system ensuring that competition in the common market is not distorted" (Article 3(f), referring to Articles 85 *et seq.*). Complementary to the free movement of goods are, of course, the three other freedoms (movement of persons, services and capital: Article 3(c)).

Particular attention should also be paid to Article 3(h); "the approximation of the laws of Member States to the extent required for the proper functioning of the Common Market." Approximation of laws will also be necessary to achieve the approximation of economic policies inasmuch as economic policy of the Member States is of a regulatory kind. The prohibition of quantitive restrictions and measures having equivalent effect (Article 3(f); Articles 30–36), the prohibition of anti-competitive behaviour influencing inter-State trade of market participants (Articles 85–86) and of the Member States (Articles 90, 92–94) and the task of the Community to harmonise legislation (Article 3(h): Article 100) must contribute to the same objective: the creation of a common market. They not only

---

[3] Pelkmans, J., "The Consumer and Market Integration in the European Community," *European Consumer Law*, p. 122.
[4] For a recent analysis by manufacturers, consumers and the Commission: *Europe* No. 3583 (April 8, 1983), p. 6–8.
[5] Kapteyn, P.J.C.—VerLoren van Themaat, P., *Inleiding tot het recht van de Europese Gemeenschappen* (3rd ed.) Deventer, 1980, p. 55.
[6] Bourgoignie, Th., n. 2 *ante*, p. 32.

share a common purpose. The underlying philosophy is one of market integration thanks to free competition.[7]

The question as to whether the consumer interest can be taken into account otherwise than indirectly as an expected result of free competition in a common market arises under Articles 30 *et seq.*, Articles 85 *et seq.* and Article 100. Under Article 85(3) a restrictive agreement can be authorised by the Commission if the advantages of the restraint of competition benefit consumers.[8]

Under Article 30 (rule of reason; see further) and Article 36 (health protection) consumer protection can be invoked to legitimate national regulations which hamper the free movement of goods. But still the consumer interest in these articles is understood as an aspect of a more general public interest.

The question asked at the beginning of this subsection is important. The existence of market failures cannot be denied. If the market has to operate on a European level, community law has to develop rules to match market failures. Considering the nature of the EEC, these rules are normally rules of an economic regulation kind (*i.e.* tolerance of restrictive practices). Such type of rules may include the tolerance of "social regulation"—the elimination of market externalities—by *Member States*.[9] The competence of the EEC institutions to issue social regulation (mainly a question of Article 100) will not be considered here.

In the aggregate a definition of the consumer interest in less or more free movement of goods is not possible. Even in a particular case it may be hard to weigh the economic interest of consumers (say, in lower prices) against their interest—or the interest of a particular class of consumers—in better protection against poor quality, health danger, confusion with other products, undue marketing influence, etc. The balance may appear to be very difficult when long term benefits have to be weighed against short term benefits.

Defining the consumer interest in respect of the application of Articles 30 *et seq.* raises the question of the competence of the Commission and the Court to question what the Member States consider to be in the interest of consumers. It will appear from the following that this questioning is only *indirect*, in that they will only look if the restrictive measure can be justified as being necessary for a defined goal (of consumer protection).

First, I would like to give a short survey of the case law on free movement of goods with special reference to consumer protection; then I shall try to draw some implications from it for national and European consumer law and policy

---

[7] Cf. the "osmose" of the different articles cited: Kapteyn—VerLoren van Themaat, n. 5 *ante*, p. 241.
[8] Evans, A., "European Competition Law and Consumers: Article 85(3) Exemption", 1981 E.C.L.R. 425.
[9] On "social regulation" and "economic regulation": in relation to "market failure," see Mitnick, Barry M., "The Political Economy of Regulation," Columbia, 1980.

PART II: "CASSIS DE DIJON," BEFORE AND AFTER

Since the preliminary ruling of the Court of Justice on February 20, 1979 in Case 120/78 *Rewe* v. *Bundesmonopolamt für Branntwein*, better known as "*Cassis de Dijon*,"[10] nearly 50 judgments relating expressly to Articles 30–36 have been given[11] and a great number of cases are pending.[12]

As Advocate General VerLoren van Themaat[13] pointed out rightly, the new wave of case law on Articles 30–36 does not start with the *Cassis de Dijon* case (Case 120/79) but with *Dassonville*.[14] The basic rule on and concept of "measures of equivalent effect," prohibited by Article 30, is to be found in ruling No. 5 of the *Dassonville* judgment.[15]

"All trading rules enacted by Member States, which are capable of hindering, directly or indirectly, actually or potentially, intra-Community trade are to be considered as measures having an effect equivalent to quantitative restrictions."

By this ruling the Court chose at least in relation to import restrictions (for export restrictions see further under Part IV) the most extensive of the three concepts[16] advanced in literature.[17] The most narrow view (Seidel, Graf, Marx) considered that only "*distinctly applicable*" measures, *i.e.* those which apply to *imported products only* (formal discrimination) fell under the notion of measures of equivalent effect.[18] The intermediate opinion, as expressed in Directive 70/50,[19] considered overtly discriminatory measures as automatically prohibited, whereas "*indistinctly applicable*" measures (governing the marketing of products which deal in particular with shape, size, weight, composition, presentation, identification or putting up and

---

[10] [1979] E.C.R. 649.
[11] See list in Appendix.
[12] See especially: Cases 314–316/81 and 83/83 (*Waterkeyn*), Cases 340 and 341/82 (cubical form margarine packets in Belgium and France).
[13] La libre circulation des Marchandises aprés l'arrêt *Cassis de Dijon, Cahiers de Droit Européen*, 1982, p. 123. See also: Kapteyn—VerLoren van Themaat, n. 5, p. 25.
[14] Case 8/74, *Procureur de Roi* v. *Dassonville* [1974], E.C.R. 837.
[15] See also Oliver, P., *Free Movement of Goods in the E.E.C. under Articles 30 to 36 of the Rome Treaty*, London, 1982, p. 60.
[16] For a summary see Van Gerven, W.—Gotzen, F., "L'élimination des barriéres non tarifaires avec référence particuliére au droit de la propriété industrielle ainsi qu'au droit d'auteur," *F.I.D.E. Reports for the Tenth Congress*, June 24–26 1981, Dublin, 1982, p. 1.1; Loewenheim, U., "Deutscher Landesbericht," *F.I.D.E. Reports*, Dublin, 1982, p. 4.3–4.5.; Oliver, P., n. 15 *ante* p. 66–67.
[17] See Ehlermann, Cl.-D., "Das Verbot der Massnahmen gleicher Wirkung in der Rechtsprechung des Gerichtshofes in *Hamburg Deutschland Europa. Feschtschrift Ipsen*, 1977, 588; Van Gerven, W., n. 16 above, p. 1.2.; Reich, N., Community Consumer Law: authorative Power of the European Commission and the Role of the Court of Justice with regard to consumer Law and Policy, in *European Consumer Law*, n. 2 *ante*, p. 229.
[18] See references in Oliver, P., n. 15 *ante*, p. 67.
[19] Commission Directive of December 22, 1969, J.O. 1970 L 13/29.

which are *equally applicable to domestic and imported products*) were lawful *unless* "the restrictive effect of such measures on the free movement of goods exceeded the effects intrinsic to trade rules."[20] Both views seem to have to be rejected by the *Dassonville* ruling cited above.[21] The Court adopted the extensive view, maintained by M. Waelbroeck[22] and P. VerLoren van Themaat),[23] that indistinctly applicable measures are generally prohibited if they restrict intracommunity trade.

The *Cassis de Dijon* judgment confirmed this basic view on the concept of measures of equivalent effect[24] and at the same time it worked out the general "exception" to the prohibition under Article 30, which the Dutch literature calls the "rule of reason."[25] This exception to, or better interpretation of, Article 30 was briefly formulated in *Dassonville*, but was defined in more detail in *Cassis de Dijon* and the subsequent judgments.

In *Dassonville* it was said:

"In the absence of a community system (guaranteeing for consumers the authenticity of a product's designation of origin), Member States may take measures to prevent unfair practices in this connexion; it is, however, subject to the condition that those measures should be reasonable."

The *Cassis de Dijon* judgment concerned a preliminary question referred to the Court on the compatibility with Article 30 of a provision of German law fixing a minimum alcohol content (25 per cent.) for fruit liqueurs. Rewe was not allowed by the German administration to import French "Cassis de Dijon" with an alcohol content of less than 25 per cent. The Court ruled that:

"Obstacles to movement within the Community resulting from disparities between the national laws relating to the marketing of the products in question must be accepted in so far as those provisions may be recognised as being necessary in order to satisfy mandatory requirements relating in particular to the effectiveness of fiscal supervision, the protection of public health, the fairness of commercial transactions and the defence of the consumer."

[20] Variants of the intermediate view were defended by Ulmer, P., "Zum Verbot mittelbarer Einführungs-beschränkungen im EWG Vertrag," *G.R.U.R. Int.*, 1975, 502 *et seq.*, and Steindorff, "Dienstleistungs-freiheit und 'ordre public' in *Dienstleistungsfreiheit und Versicherungsaufsicht im Gemeinsamen Markt*, 1971, p. 79 *et seq.*
[21] See n. 17 *ante*.
[22] Megret, J.—Louis, J.-V.—Vignes, D.—Waelbroeck, M., *Le Droit de le Communauté Economique Européenne*, Vol. 1, 2° tirage, Bruxelles, 1973, p. 102.
[23] "*Bevat artikel 30 van het E.E.G.-Verdrag slechts een non-discriminatiebeginsel t.a.v. invoerbeperkingen?*" *S.E.W.*, 1967, p. 362; "E.E.G.-richtlijnen betreffende . . . ," *S.E.W.*, 1970, p. 258.
[24] VerLoren van Themaat, note 13, *ante*, No. 2–3; Barents, R., "New Developments in Measures having Equivalent Effect," 1981 C.M.L. Rev. 271 *et seq.*; Van Gerven, W., n. 16 *ante*, p. 1.6.
[25] See Barents, R., n. 24 *ante*, p. 284.

It rejected the arguments of the German government to the effect that the 25 per cent. standard was justified on grounds of public health and consumer protection. A prohibition against marketing "Cassis de Dijon" was not considered to be necessary for the goal of consumer protection pursued by the German government (protection against confusion): a labelling requirement would have been a sufficient guarantee.

Cassis de Dijon was the first of a series of Cases on Articles 30–36 with special relevance to consumer protection. Indeed, it first explicitly raised the question of whether Member States are entitled to impose higher standards of safety, quality and labelling for consumer goods than other Member States.

The *Cassis de Dijon* "rule of reason" was repeated in a number of cases. With respect to consumer protection this rule of reason and some of the exceptions listed exhaustively in Article 36 will be considered in more detail later.

The importance of the *Cassis de Dijon* case was recognised by the Commission when it made its statement "concerning the consequences of the judgment . . . ."[26] In this statement it was said that "the Commission will have to tackle a whole body of commercial rules which lay down that products manufactured and marketed in one Member State must fulfil technical or qualitative conditions in order to be admitted to the market of another and specifically in all cases where the trade barriers occasioned by such rules are inadmissible according to the *very strict criteria* set out by the Court" (emphasis added). The "very strict criteria" the Commission refers to are explained as the *necessity* of the rule in order to satisfy mandatory requirements (*inter alia* consumer protection) of *general interest* compelling enough to justify an exception to the free movement of goods, and the *proportionality* (most appropriate means which at the same time least hinder trade).

As to the exact meaning of the *Cassis de Dijon* case, some general questions remained and some still remain, even after a large number of cases on similar matters:

(1) The relationships between Articles 30 and 36, especially the possibility of justification of "distinctly applicable" (overtly discriminatory) measures;

(2) The requirement of "discrimination" for the concept of measures of equivalent effect (albeit a presumed discrimination);

(3) The exact meaning of *"lawfully produced and marketed"* in consideration 14 of the *Cassis de Dijon* judgment ("There is therefore no valid reason, why, provided that they have been lawfully produced and marketed in one of the Member

---

[26] O.J. 1982 C256/3. For criticism on form and content of this letter, see Barents, R., note 24 *ante*, p. 296.

States, alcohol beverages should not be introduced into any other Member State").

(4) The significance of the words "*in the absence of common rules relating to the production and marketing of alcohol* . . . it is for the Member States to regulate all matters relating to the production and marketing (of alcohol etc.)" in consideration 8 of the *Cassis de Dijon* judgment.

The third and fourth question will be discussed in "consumer protection" and "protection of health and life of humans," *post*. As to the first question, it may suffice to mention that in Case 113/80 (*Commission* v. *Ireland*) the Court gave the clear answer that *Cassis de Dijon* and later cases only relate to provisions which regulate in a uniform manner the marketing of domestic products and imported products[27] (*i.e.* "indistinctly applicable measures").

As to the second question, it seems useful to start by mentioning the view of Timmermans[28] that the "rule of reason" developed by the Court under Article 20 has (almost) the same effect as the concept of *material* discrimination (*i.e.* equal treatment of unequal cases which leads to a discriminatory effect) which occurs in relation to other community law questions. Further, there is evidence that a measure which is not "indistinctly" applicable, but applies only to foreign products is not necessarily discriminatory (in a material sense). This can be the case with the indication of the foreign origin of a product, if that origin implies a certain (poorer) quality.[29] In any case, the question may remain whether a distinctly applicable (thus formally discriminatory) measure can be justified under the "rule of reason" (when it does not discriminate materially) as well as under Article 36 (which only prohibits "arbitrary discrimination").

Originally, it was quite generally[30] admitted that *Cassis de Dijon* implied that while discrimination may be sufficient to establish an infringement of Article 30,[31] it is not necessary; in other words, "the test was not whether a measure discriminates (in substance) against imports, but whether it *restricts* imports."[32]

In the *Blesgen* case (75/81), however, the Advocate General held that the concept of "measure of equivalent effect" only covered *de jure* or *de facto* discrimination. The Court followed his view and, with reference to Article 3, Directive 70/50, held that indistinctly applicable measures fall under Article 30, *provided* that their restrictive effect on the free movement of goods exceeds the effects intrinsic to trade rules.

---

[27] See Gravelli, Nigel, P., Review of Oliver's book (n. 15 *ante*), 1983 E.L.Rev. 79–80.
[28] "Verboden discriminatie of geboden differentiatie," 1982 S.E.W. 453–455.
[29] *Cf.* consideration 13 of Case 113/80 (*Commission* v. *Ireland*).
[30] See Oliver, P., n. 15, *ante*, with further references.
[31] See *e.g.* Case 193/80 (*Commission* v. *Italy*).
[32] Oliver, P., n. 15, *ante*, p. 70.

Recalling Timmermans' thesis that the "rule of reason" of *Cassis de Dijon* (with its elements of proportionality and justification: see below) does not essentially differ from the notion of material discrimination, the question whether discrimination, after *Blesgen*, would indeed[33] seem to be a necessary, but presumed element for a *Cassis de Dijon* infringement, whenever the sale of goods in free circulation in one Member State is prohibited in another,[34] is not so important. However, the *Blesgen* case certainly casts doubts on the continued reliability of the *Dassonville* formula, according to which even measures having only an *indirect* effect on inter-state trade fall under the scope of Article 30.[35]

Moreover, if the *Blesgen* jurisprudence is to be continued we might be back in a pre-*Dassonville* situation. Therefore, as in Directive 70/50, only a restrictive effect which *exceeds* the effects intrinsic to "trade rules" makes "indistinctly" (not overtly discriminatory) applicable measures fall within the prohibition of Article 20, whereas "*Cassis de Dijon*" mentioned only a "restrictive" (albeit discriminatory) *effect*.

Blesgen raises the question as to the meaning of "trade rules," nowhere precisely defined (but see the last but one paragraph of Part II) and brings into the debate the second part of Article 3, Directive 70/50, in which it is said that this (the excessively restrictive effect) is the case, where the restrictive effects on the free movement of goods are out of proportion to their purpose and the same objective can be attained by other means which are less of a hindrance to trade.

This is in fact a way to formulate the *proportionality* principle, well known from the established jurisprudence of the Court,[36] and part of the "rule of reason" (see "protection of health and life of humans," *post*).

Summarised, the main problem with *Blesgen* was that it denied an import restrictive effect to a (not formally discriminatory) measure, on the ground that it did not have a direct connection with imports and that the reference to Article 3, Directive 70/50, might be interpreted as a return to the rule laid down in that Directive whereby the burden of proof of illegality is borne by the party challenging an indistinctly applicable measure.

In any case, the apparent swing in jurisprudence in *Blesgen* should not be dramatised. In the light of the facts of the case (the limited effect of the Belgian "loi Vandervelde" on the import of strong alcoholic beverages) it has been argued that *Blesgen* could be interpreted as the introduction of a *de minimis* rule into the free movement of goods

---

[33] As argued by Wyatt, D., "Article 30 and non-discriminatory Trade Restrictions", 1981 E.L.Rev. 189–193. This author, however, also includes material discrimination (*cf.* Timmermans, n. 28, *ante*).
[34] Such as suggested by Gravelli, n. 27, *ante cf.* the comment on the case by Arnull, Anthony, M., 1982 E.L.Rev. 393 *et seq*.
[35] Arnull, n. 34 *ante*, p. 398.
[36] See especially Case 104/75, *De Peijper* [1976] E.C.R. 613.

jurisprudence, comparable with the one existing in relation to Article 85.[37]

As it is, the prohibition of "measures of equivalent effect"in Article 30 still covers a whole range of national measures, a prohibition not only mitigated by the exhaustive list of grounds of justification in Article 36, but also by the "rule of reason"under Article 30 (see further under Part III).

"Measures of equivalent effect on imports" cover "all trading rules" (Case 8/74, *Dassonville*), *i.e.* regulations about marketing as well as production and consumption (Case 788/79, *Gilli and Andres;* Case 113/80, *Commission* v. *Ireland*).

Since Case 249/81 (*Commission* v. *Ireland*), it is clear that national measures without legal effect (such as a campaign to buy domestic products) are covered.

PART III: THE "RULE OF REASON" AND ARTICLE 36

P. Oliver supports the view that *Cassis de Dijon* and later cases, in which no reference to Article 36 is made and which accept obstacles to the free movement of goods justified by mandatory requirements of general interest (which are not mentioned in Article 36), are to be considered as extensions of the list of grounds of justification set out in Article 36.[38] Thus all measures (whether "distinctly" or "indistinctly applicable") would be subject to the same twofold test: 1) does the measure restrict imports (Article 36); 2) if so, is it justified under Article 36 as extended by *Cassis de Dijon* ("mandatory requirements").

I am inclined to follow the other view, espoused by P. VerLoren van Themaat,[39] that "distinctly applicable measures" can only be justified on the grounds expressly enumerated in Article 36, whereas "indistinctly applicable measures" may be justified under a "rule of reason." The rule of reason (or "reasonable measures clause"[40]) under Article 30 and the exceptions of Article 36 have to be kept separate. This view is more consistent with the Court's ruling that "distinctly applicable" measures can only be justified on the grounds expressly enumerated in Article 36, whereas "indistinctly applicable" measures may be justified under the *Cassis de Dijon* jurispru-

---

[37] Waelbroeck, Didier, Comments on Cases 75/81 (*Blesgen*) and 220/81 (*Robertson*), *Cahiers de Droit Européen*, 1983, 247; the de minimis rule (no infringement when the influence on inter-state trade is negligible) is well established in competition law since Case 5/69, *Völk/Vervaecke* [1969] E.C.R. 295. Michel Waelbroeck, on the contrary, rejects the idea of a *de minimis* rule and refers to Case 24/68, *Commission* v. *Italy* [1969] E.C.R. 1963, concerning taxes of equivalent effect: "Mesures d'effet équivalent, discrimination formelle et matérielle dans la jurisprudence de la Cour de Justice," in *Liber Amicorum F. Dumon*, Antwerp, 1983, p. 1355.
[38] Oliver, P., n. 15, *ante*, p. 73.
[39] N. 13, *ante*.
[40] Terminology proposed by Barents, R., n. 24, *ante*, p. 248.

dence. It should be stressed however that the criteria the Court uses under both Articles 36 and 30 (under which the *Cassis de Dijon* rule of reason is subsumed) are comparable.

A. Article 36: the exceptions

Logically, when a national measure is challenged because of its restrictive effect on imports, the first test is Article 36. Indeed, as stated earlier, under Article 36 a measure may be justified even if it is "distinctly applicable" (*i.e.* formally discriminatory or discriminatory by nature for imported goods). Moreover, as Article 36 explicitly enumerates grounds for justification, a prima facie justification (*e.g.* "health of humans" in relation to sanitary inspection) is more likely to occur than under the "rule of reason" and will at least *de facto* switch the burden of proof in relation to the presence or absence of justification to the party challenging the measure.

Under Article 36 the measure has to be "justified on grounds of public morality, public policy or public security, the protection of health and life of humans, animals or plants, the protection of national treasures possessing artistic, historic or archaeological value; or the protection of industrial and commercial property. Such prohibitions or restrictions shall not, however, constitute a means of arbitrary discrimination or a disguised restriction on trade between Member States." *The list of grounds is exhaustive.*[41]

Examples of arbitrary discrimination, which is never authorised, can be found in Cases 152/78 (French alcohol advertising), 34/79 (import restrictions on pornography in the U.K.), 104/75[42] (discrimination on parallel imports of drugs) and 40/82 (*Commission* v. *U.K.*: public health measures on poultry imports in the U.K.). Examples of disguised protectionism can be found in Cases 34/79 and 40/82, both cited.

As the difference (in the Court's jurisprudence cited) between mere discrimination—*i.e.* the difference between the applicability of laws to domestic and imported goods and their applicability only to the latter—and "arbitrary" discrimination is not very clear, and certainly not great, the possibility of distinctly applicable measures escaping from the prohibition of Article 30 by invoking Article 36 will certainly remain quite small. Distinctly applicable measures which are not necessarily arbitrarily discriminatory (nor a cloak for protectionist measures) will be found in relation to health controls (*e.g.* of foodstuffs) at the Member States' borders.[43] A genuine meaning of "arbitrary discrimination" in the last sentence of Article 36 seems to be the prohibition of the discriminatory *application* of indistinctly

---

[41] See Case 95/81, *Commission* v. *Italy* [1982] E.C.R. 2187.
[42] *De Peijper* [1976] E.C.R. 613.
[43] See Case 132/80 *United Foods* v. *Belgium*; 40/82, *Commission* v. *U.K.*; and explicitly: Case 124/81 *Commission* v. *U.K.* But in the three cases cited Article 36 *in casu* applied.

applicable measures[44] or the discriminatory exercise of industrial property rights which by nature have a territorial effect.

A justification under Article 36 will only be possible under one of the grounds listed, which are designed for situations of a *non-economic nature*[45] and do not expressly mention *consumer protection*.

Both restrictions on the applicability of Article 36 need some comment. The first restriction, the "non-economic nature," also applies to the "rule of reason;" only there it can lead to important interpretation problems because of the open nature of the rule of reason. It will be discussed in relation to that rule (see under B). The exclusion of consumer protection concerns only Article 36. In the "rule of reason" as formulated in *Cassis de Dijon* (Case 120/78), as well as in Cases such as 788/79 (*Gilli and Andres*), 130/80 (*Keldermann*) and 113/80 (*Commission v. Ireland*) consumer protection is expressly mentioned as one of the justification grounds (see more in detail under B). Furthermore two of the grounds enumerated in Article 36 are linked to consumer protection: the protection of industrial and commercial property and especially the protection of human health and life.

(1) *Protection of industrial and commercial property*

This ground of justification is of minor importance for consumer protection. In the first place, the court excludes from this category the protection against slavish imitation and unfair competition in general (Case 144/81: *Keurkoop v. Nancy Kean Gifts;* implicitly in Cases 58/80, *Dansk Supermarket v. Imercó;* and 6/81, *Industrie Diensten Groep v. Beele*).[46] This exclusion leaves doubts about the position of protection of trade names, service trade marks and indications of origin, which in some Member States belong to industrial property law and in others to unfair competition law.[47]

In the second place, the Court's case law on the applicability of Articles 30–36 to industrial property such as trade marks and patents rights[48] cannot by the very nature of these rights be considered as consumer protective.[49]

(2) *Protection of health and life of humans*

This ground of justification is, of course, very important to consumers, but it has often been used as a pretext for protectionism.

In *Cassis de Dijon* (Case 120/78)[50] the Court enumerated a number of grounds of justification under the "rule of reason" (see *ante*). One of these grounds is the protection of "public health." In

---

[44] Case 8/74, *Dassonville*, n. 14, *ante*.
[45] Well-settled case law, see recently Case 95/81, *Commission v. Italy*.
[46] See Eeckman, P., comment on *Industrie Diensten Groep* and *Keurkoop* in 1983 S.E.W. 326, 426.
[47] Eeckman, P., n. 46 *ante*, p. 426.
[48] And recently design protection: Case 144/81, *Keurkoop v. Nancy Kean Gifts*.
[49] See Stuyck, J., *Product Differentiations*, Deventer 1982, p. 109.
[50] N. 10, *ante*.

Cassis de Dijon the German government tried to justify the provisions of German law prohibiting the sale of fruit liqueur with less than 25 per cent. alcohol. Needless to say that this argument fell flat, (see consideration 11).

The protection of public health has also been rejected as a ground of justification under the "rule of reason," *i.e.* without reference to Article 36, in Cases 153/78 (*Commission* v. *Germany:* prohibition on the importation of meat-based products manufactured in one Member State from animals slaughtered in another Member State); 788/79 (*Gilli and Andres:* prohibition of vinegar other than wine vinegar); 130/80 (*Kelderman:* prohibition of bread containing more than a given quantity of dry matter); 59/82 (*Schutzverband* v. *Weinvertriebs GmbH:* import prohibition of vermouth with lower alcohol degree than the one fixed by the export country).

In Cases 152/78 (*Commission* v. *France:* advertising for alcoholic beverages) and 104/75 (*De Peijper*)[51] the justification was rejected because the measure, although possibly justified by concern for public health, was nevertheless an "arbitrary discrimination," and even more so in Case 40/82 (*Commission* v. *U.K.:* health import restrictions on poultry and eggs). But here the Court seemed to subject the second sentence of Article 36 to the proportionality test, which until now was only applied to Article 36, first sentence.[52]

It may also be recalled that the Court does not accept "public health" as a justification for the use of industrial property rights (in the area of pharmaceuticals) (Case 15/74).[53]

In fact only in Cases 53/80 (*Eyssen:* Dutch prohibition on the addition of nisin to processed cheese); 251/78 (*Denkavit*) and 272/80 (*Biologische Producten:* Dutch prohibition of the sale of plant protection products without prior government approval) did the Court accept the justification on "public health" grounds. The two latter decisions on health inspection are in line with earlier decisions.[54]

The *Eyssen* (nisin) case is more important for my subject, as it directly relates to the core of consumer health protection: foodstuff additives. Avoiding a ruling on the compatibility with Articles 30–36 of "positive lists," the Court held that the Dutch regulation was justified under Article 36—hereby disregarding the *Cassis de Dijon* rule of reason—taking into account the uncertainty as to the quantities in which nisin could be harmful. It appears from this case, in which the Court mixes up the rule of reason and Article 36, but at least summarises both,[55] that in both situations the same criteria apply. Important for the future of consumer protection, and a relief for those who feared for it after *Cassis de Dijon,* was the fact that the Court was willing to accept a consumer protection goal as justifica-

---

[51] See n. 42, *ante.*
[52] Minor, Jackie, "Turkeys: the abuse of Article 36 E.E.C.," 1983 E.L.R. 122.
[53] October 31, 1974, *Centrafarm* v. *Sterling Drug Inc.* [1974] E.C.R. 1147.
[54] Beginning with Case 104/75, *De Peijper,* n. 42; for a summary of this jurisprudence: see Barents, R., n. 24, *ante,* pp. 282–283.
[55] See comment by Keur, D.J., in 1981 S.E.W. 659.

tion, *even if it was not proved with certainty* that the national regulation was necessary for that goal. As the concept of "justification" or "necessity" seems to be the same under both Article 36 and the "rule of reason," the point is of great interest.[56] The concept will be discussed under the "rule of reason."

B. The "rule of reason" (or "reasonable measures clause")

Advocate General VerLoren Van Themaat explains[57] that the term "reasonable measures clause" is referred to in consideration 6 of the *Dassonville* case where it is said that if a Member State takes measures to prevent the unfair practices at stake, "it is however subject to the condition that these measures should be *reasonable*." The term "rule of reason" refers to the American case law on the Sherman Act where a strict prohibition of cartels is mitigated by a "rule of reason."

In respect of Article 30 the "rule of reason" is laid down by analogy with Article 36 (the most important difference being that it does not apply to "distinctly applicable measures").

Ultimately the "rule of reason," which also seems to appear in relation to Articles 59 *et seq.*, is more than an exception. It is "a general principle of interpretation for the strict provisions of the Treaty," according to the Advocate General.

The general features of the "rule of reason" of Article 30 since *Cassis de Dijon* (see *ante*) can be summarised as follows:

(i) only "indistinctly applicable" (not formally discriminatory) measures can benefit from it.
(ii) the obstacle to imports from another Member State is the result of disparities between national laws, in *the absence of community legislation* (consideration 8 of Case 120/78, *Cassis de Dijon;* more explicitly Case 148/78, *Ratti*).[58]
(iii) the national measure falls *outside the scope of economic policy*. The Court has confined the application of Article 36 to "non-economic measures," but it is agreed that this restriction also applies to the rule of reason.[59] As indicated above "economic" has to be understood in the restrictive sense of "economic policy" (promotion of employment or investment, control of inflation etc. . . .)[60] a term still subject

---

[56] See, however, Judge A. Touffait ("Les entraves techniques à la libre circulation des marchandises," *Recueil Dalloz Sirey*, 1982, chron, pp. 37 *et seq*) who is of the opinion that this and other facilities only apply to Article 36; but this opinion seems isolated: Lando, O., "General Report on Consumer Protection and the Common Market", *F.I.D.E. Reports*, Dublin, 1982, p. 104.
[57] See n. 1 to Conclusion in Case 286/81 (*Oosthoek*).
[58] For more details see Oliver, P., n. 15, *ante*, pp. 132–133.
[59] Barents, n. 24, *ante*, p. 289; VerLoren van Themaat, n. 13, *ante*, p. 10; For authors such as Oliver, P., who subsume *Cassis de Dijon* under Article 36, the generality of this requirement is not in point.
[60] Oliver, P., n. 15, *ante*, p. 134; Barents, n. 24, *ante*, p. 289.

to interpretation but letting objectives such as the protection of economic interests (*e.g.* of consumers) benefit from the rule of reason. This restriction could, of course, have an important negative effect on consumer protection inasmuch as price control (which in relation to EEC imported products is often to be considered as a measure of equivalent effect) would be genuinely in the consumer interest.[61] This very complicated question cannot be discussed here. Suffice it to say that competition policy is often considered as an alternative to public price control as in the fight against inflation and that prices and income policy are closely linked.

(iv) the measure has to be *necessary*.
(v) in order to satisfy *mandatory requirements*
(vi) relating *in particular* to the effectiveness of fiscal supervision, the protection of public health, the fairness of commercial transactions and the defence of the consumer. . . .
(vii) but the measure may in no way constitute an arbitrary discrimination or disguised restriction of trade (*Dassonville*).[62]

(1) *Comments on points (iv), (v) and (vi)*

The measure has to be *necessary*, in other words reasonable (*cf. Dassonville*), *i.e.* proportional in relation to the purposes to be protected.[63] *Proportionality* is a general principle of Community law derived from German law ("Verhältnismässigkeit").[64] The necessity must relate to mandatory requirements, *serving a purpose of general interest*. The words in italics figure in the Commission's Communication,[65] but there is no doubt that they are implied by the non-exhaustive enumerations given in the Court's decisions.[66]

(2) *Fairness of commercial transactions*

A measure may be justified in order to prevent unfair competition. As the law against unfair competition in some countries, especially in Germany, takes into account the consumer interest,[67]

---

[61] On the complex question of price control in relation to Article 30, see Colinet, C., and Marescau, M." Interprétation et application du droit communautaire dans le domaine des règlementations de prix des produits agricoles," 1980 *Cah. Dr. Eur.* 507.
[62] This is identical to the last sentence of Article 36.
[63] See, in this respect, the second part of Article 3, Directive 70/50 cited *ante*, and the following passages from the Commission's Communication concerning *Cassis de Dijon*, O.J. 1980 C256/2: "appropriate and not excessive."
[64] Hartley, T.C., *The Foundations of European Community Law*, Oxford 1981, p. 137.
[65] See n. 26, *ante*.
[66] The purposes of general interest enumerated by the Court are not exhaustive. So far this enumeration includes the protection of public health, the fairness of commercial transactions and the defence of the consumer.
[67] Schricker, G., "Unfair Competition and Consumer Protection in Western Europe, 1970 1 I.I.C. p. 415; Baumbach-Hefermehl, *Wettbewerksrecht*, (13th ed.) München 1981, p. 177; 193–194.

this ground of justification is examined here.[68] Three cases after *Cassis de Dijon* relate to unfair competition in the broad sense, as defined in Article 10 of the Paris Convention and in the literature[69]: Cases 58/80 (*Dansk Supermarket* v. *Imerco*), 6/81 (*Industrie Diensten Groep* v. *Beele*), 261/81 (*Oosthoek*).

In Case 58/80 the Court stated that "Community law does not in principle have the effect of preventing the application in a Member State to goods imported from other Member States of the provision on marketing in force in the State of importation. It follows that the marketing of imported goods may be prohibited if the conditions on which they are sold *constitute an infringement of the marketing usages considered proper and fair in the Member State of importation*" (author's italics). This means that each Member State can, as long as unfair competition law is not harmonised, define in a different way what it regards as unfair competition, with this evident restriction "that *the importation* into a Member State of goods lawfully marketed in another Member State cannot *as such* be classified as an improper or unfair commercial practice, without prejudice however to the possible application of legislation of the state of importation against such practices on the ground of the circumstances or methods of offering such goods for sale as distinct from the actual fact of importation."

In Case 6/81 the Court naturally accepted that it was justified, on the grounds of the prevention of unfair competition and consumer protection against confusion, in prohibiting the sale of imported goods which were a slavish imitation of other goods marketed in the import country over a long period of time.

The more recent Case 286/81 (*Oosthoek*) related to the compatibility with Article 30 of the Dutch legislation on premium offers (Wet Beperking Cadeaustelsel 1977). A provision of this Act requiring a "consumption connection" between the product and the premium made it impossible for a Dutch-Belgian publisher to offer a free dictionary to Dutch purchasers of his encyclopaedia whereas this was possible under Belgian law.

The Dutch provision could stand the test of Article 30, if it could be justified on the grounds of consumer protection and/or fair trading. The Advocate-General VerLoren van Themaat shows in his observations that the Act is aimed at the protection of fairness in trade. A second aim of the Act is the promotion of "good economic order" (orderlijk economisch verkeer). In its opinion to the Court the Commission supported the view that all measures aimed at the promotion of good economic order—as distinct from measures of

---

[68] *Cf.*: In an earlier decision (Case 12/74, *Commission* v. *Germany* [1975] E.C.R. 181) which is overruled by Case 58/80 (discussed below) the Court stated that a measure might only be justified on the grounds of unfair competition if it was simultaneously justified on the grounds of consumer protection.

[69] See Ulmer, E., *Das Recht des unlauteren Wettbewerbs in den Mitgliedstaaten des EWG, Band I, Vergleichende Darstellung.*

economic policy, aimed at the realisation of economic goals—are to be considered as falling under the "rule of reason."

The Court does not go into this argument, and states that "the provision of the Dutch Act at stake contributes to the protection of the consumer and fairness of commercial transactions. The concept "fairness of commercial transactions" thus seems to include unfair competition law as well as legislation on a good economic order, such as regulations on auction sales, clearance sales, premium offers etc. This seems natural; though in Holland these subjects seem to be a separate field of law, generally on the continent they are considered to be integrated with unfair competition law.[70]

Nevertheless it would be interesting to learn what the Court would decide on the compatibility of a number of other national regulations in the field of unfair competition, trade practices and advertising considered by the national legislator as being in the interest of consumers and/or fairness in commercial transactions, but which are *in fact* aimed at protecting specific categories of local traders, *e.g.* small shopkeepers, against certain forms of competition (not only unfair competition) from others. An example is the prohibition of itinerant sales, *i.e.* sales in hired rooms, by Article 53, Belgian Trade Practices Act 1971, which is likely to hamper direct sales from other Member States.[71]

(3) *Consumer Protection*

Since *Cassis de Dijon* it is clear that, in the absence of Community legislation, genuine goals of consumer protection[72] justify national measures having a restrictive effect on imports (but treating domestic and imported products indiscriminately), if these measures are necessary, *i.e.* proportional to their purpose and the same result is not likely to be attained with less restrictive measures. This reasonableness test in respect of consumer protection has been explicated by the principle that *the sale of a product should never be prohibited when the consumer will be sufficently protected by adequate labelling requirements.*[73] This principle can be found in Case 120/78. (*Cassis de Dijon*) and more expressly in Case 53/80 (*Fietje*).

Another principle of importance here is the *principle of equivalence*[74]: if the product meets the standards of the Member State of export which are equivalent (*i.e.* have the *same* consumer protective effect) it may not be prohibited in the Member State of import on the grounds that it does not meet the standards of this Member State. In Case 53/80 (*Fietje*) the Court decided that a labelling

---

[70] See Ulmer, E., n. 69 *ante*, pp. 211–230.
[71] For an example see Court of Appeal of Antwerp, December 17, 1980, 1982 *Jurisprudence Commerciale de Belgique*, p. 50, observations from Stuyck, J.
[72] Consumer protection was not real in Cases 120/78 (*Cassis de Dijon*), 788/79 (*Gilli and Andres*), 193/80 (*Commission* v. *Italy*), 261/81 (*Rau*), 94/82 (*De Kikvorsch*).
[73] Oliver, P., n. 15, *ante*, p. 147, calls this principle the "golden rule."
[74] Term used by Oliver, P., n. 15, *ante*, and especially in "Measures of equivalent Effect: a Reappraisal," 1982 *C.M.L.Rev.* pp. 234–237.

requirement was not justified where the imported goods already had a label containing at least the same information in a form which the consumer could understand equally well. This is the meaning of the problematic addition in the dictum in *Cassis de Dijon* "[There is therefore no valid reason, why,] provided that they have been lawfully produced and marketed in one of the Member States [alcohol beverages should . . .]".[75]

In Case 220/81 (*Robertson:* preliminary ruling on the Belgian hallmarking of silver) this doctrine was repeated and the Court added that the establishment of the equivalence is the task of the national Court which has to take into account the elements of interpretation specified by the Court.

PART IV: ARTICLE 34 AND EXPORTS

Measures of equivalent effect on exports (Article 34) are basically governed by the same principle as measures of equivalent effect on imports. For that reason, and as their significance for consumer protection is not so great, I shall be very short.

The most important difference between Articles 30 and 34 seems to be that the latter article would only prohibit measures with a *discriminatory* restrictive effect on exports, in other words, which are *distinctly* applicable to domestic production for domestic use and domestic production for export trade[76]; or in the words of the Court: "national measures which have as their specific object or effect the restriction of patterns of exports and thereby the establishment of a difference between the domestic trade of a Member State and its export trade in such a way as to favour national production or the domestic market (Case 15/79, *Groenveld;* Case 155/80, *Oebel;* Case 141–143/81, *Holdijk*). However, all judgments cited relate to restrictions on *production* (prohibition on producing horse meat, prohibition on baking at night, protection of fattening calves). Whether this principle is also applicable to restrictions on sale is debatable[77] even after Case 29/82 (*Luipen*).

PART V: IMPLICATIONS FOR NATIONAL AND EUROPEAN CONSUMER LAW AND POLICY

A. Implications for national consumer law and policy

(1) *In general*

(a) The main effect of the *Cassis de Dijon* decision is that consumer protection will never be accepted as a pretext for protectionism.

---

[75] See Barents, R., n. 24, *ante*, p. 296, who compares this phrase to the *Dassonville* case ("put in free circulation in a regular manner").
[76] VerLoren van Themaat, P., "De artikelen 30–36 van het EEG-Verdrag," *R.M. Themis*, 1980, p. 378; *contra:* Oliver P., n. 15, *ante*, p. 82.
[77] Oliver, P., n. 15, *ante*, p. 83, is of the opinion that *Cassis de Dijon* applies here. A.G. Gordon Slynn leaves the question open in *Holdijk* [1982] E.C.R. 1320.

(b) By denouncing "false consumer policy"[78] the Court and the Commission support genuine consumer policy, which to the extent that there are no Community rules[79] remains a matter of national competence.

(c) Where common rules exist (*e.g.* harmonisation under Article 100), as is the case for quality standards and labelling requirements for a number of foodstuffs, Member States cannot invoke the "rule of reason" or Article 36 in order to justify the application of additional requirements to products imported from other Member States, unless these national requirements are established in accordance with these common rules (Case 148/78, *Ratti*).

As harmonisation directives in the consumer area—or proposals for such directives—very often contain only minimum requirements,[80] the *Ratti* doctrine should not matter too much. Directives on foodstuffs (composition) normally establish total approximation (*i.e.* no additional requirements even for domestic products). Nevertheless they leave certain points to the competence of the Member States.[81] In the only "consumer" directive already in force—the foodstuffs labelling, presentation and advertising Directive,[82]—the authority for Member States to apply additional labelling requirements seems to be subject to a *Cassis de Dijon* kind of test. Article 15 of the Directive reads:

"1. Member States may not forbid trade in foodstuffs which comply with the rules laid down in this Directive by the application of non-harmonised national provisions governing the labelling and presentation of certain foodstuffs or of foodstuffs in general.
2. Paragraph 1 shall not apply to non-harmonised national provisions justified on grounds of:
—protection of public health,
—prevention of fraud, unless such provisions are liable to impede the application of the definitions and rules laid down by this Directive,
—protection of industrial and commercial property rights, indications of provenance, registered designations of origin and prevention of unfair competition."

It should, however, be said that when reference is made to this article the Member State has to notify the proposed measure to the Commission and may not adopt the measure, if the Commission

---

[78] Reich, N., n. 17 *ante*, p. 223.
[79] But see on "the non-legislative role of the European Commission towards integration of consumer law and policy": Freedman, S. in *European Consumer Law*, n. 2 *ante*, pp. 291–303.
[80] Krämer, L., *Les Consommateurs et l'Europe*, Brussels 1978, pp. 186–187.
[81] Krämer, L. n. 80, *ante*, p. 184.
[82] 79/112 EEC, O.J. 1979 L 33/1.

gives a negative opinion (to be delivered within three months after reference to the Standing Committee on Foodstuffs) (Articles 16–17). The first example of such a veto of the Commission is the Decision of July 22, 1983 requesting Belgium to suspend certain labelling requirements in a draft of a decree relating to manufactured meat.[83] The Commission considered in this decision that the measure proposed by the Belgian government (mandatory impression of the words "non edible" on bowls of synthetic material) was not necessary because the information for the consumer could be given at least as efficiently by other means.

(d) Where Member State A has a stricter, more protective rule, Member State B cannot require that products originating from Member State A conform to the stricter standard applicable for domestic sale in A. This rule can be derived from Case 59/82 (*Schutzverband* v. *Weinvertriebs-GmbH*).

(e) In the absence of a common rule a Member State may establish product standards (*e.g.* quality standards) for domestic products.[84] In her opinion in Case 83/82 *Waterkeyn* Advocate General Rozes put forward the view that *negative discrimination, i.e.* hampering domestic production and sale as a result of a national rule not applicable to imported products, is not prohibited in relation to the free movement of goods. The Court was not asked to give an opinion on this question of interpretation of Article 7. Asked about the interpretation of its decision in Case 152/78 (*Commission* v. *France*) the Court quite naturally answered that in the latter decision the French alcohol advertising regulation has only been declared incompatible with Article 30 in so far as it contains less advantageous provisions in relation to products imported from other Member Countries.

(f) Until now case law has not tackled the question whether products originating from third countries but put into free circulation in one Member State may only be prevented from being imported into other Member States under the *Cassis de Dijon* conditions.

(g) The most important general conclusion for national consumer law is that *Cassis de Dijon as such* does not necessarily lead to a lowering of standards and to a situation where some manufacturers would chose the Member State with the lowest standard as the place of production for the European market. Indeed the "rule of reason" and the "necessity" under Article 36 imply that if a Member State adopts a higher level of consumer protection, it can impose on producers and sellers throughout the Community who want to sell their products in that Member Country obligations concerning safety, labelling,

---

[83] O.J. 1983 L. 218/16.
[84] Case 204/80, *Procureur de la République* v. *Vedel*, [1982] E.C.R. 465.

quality *etc.* which reasonably speaking are necessary to reach that higher level.

Fear about the future of consumer protection after *Cassis de Dijon* was especially expressed in relation to the Commission's communication (cited). The fifth paragraph of this communication read: "*Any product lawfully produced and marketed in one Member State, must, in principle be admitted to the market of any other Member State*" where the Court would only have made a condition of the lawful production and marketing for admission to the import State and only after having decided that the prohibition of the products constituted a measure of equivalent effect. Apart from the fact that the "lawful production *etc.*" is not even a condition in the jurisprudence of the Court (see note 75), the criticism was justified, although in fact there was only a shift in emphasis. The Court accepted the application of national law provided a valid reason existed; the Commission seems to presume that normally there is no valid reason. A justified fear may exist in relation to the apparent underlying policy swing of the Commission in the direction of more non-legislative consumer protection and less harmonisation, as also expressed in the second consumer programme.[85]

Originally, the strict way in which this "necessity" was established, *i.e.* by the Court of Justice itself (see *Cassis de Dijon*) could be frustrating for national consumer policy, but later cases have shown that this only applies to obvious situations. In Case 53/80 *Eyssen* uncertainty about health risks led to acceptance of the national provision. In Case 220/81 *Robertson* (hallmarking of silver) the Court even decided that it was up to the national Court (requesting a preliminary ruling) to evaluate this "necessity." Moreover the Court has never (see (b) above) questioned national *goals* of consumer protection themselves (*e.g.* in respect of fairness of trade, *ante*).

(h) Finally, it could be deduced from decisions of the Court of Justice in relation to other Treaty provisions (*e.g.* Case 45/76)[86] that even private persons could be bound by Article 30 *et seq.* Barents, who supports this view, gives an example of a trade union boycott of certain foreign products.[87]

(2) *Implications for specific branches of consumer law.*

(a) **Labelling law.** Labelling law as such may have a revival, as labelling is often the least import-restrictive alternative for compulsory product minimum standards. Labelling requirements must of course be "necessary." Labelling in the language of the importing

---

[85] On the non-legislative approach, see: European Consumer Law Group, "Non legislative Means of Consumer Protection," 1983 6 J.C.P. pp. 209–230. For a "pessimistic" interpretation of the Court's jurisprudence and a proposal of an alternative to the "new economic policy" of the EEC see Micklitz, "Technische Normen, Produzentenhaftung und EWG-Vertrag," 1983 N.J.W. pp. 483 *et seq.*
[86] *Comet* v. *Produktschap voor Siergewassen*, [1976] E.C.R. 2043.
[87] n. 24, *ante*, p. 275, n. 17.

country is not always necessary (Case 17/80 *Fietje*) to inform the consumer in a proper way.[88]

As to the specific and actual question as to whether a Member State may impose the indication of the country of origin for products originating from another Member State, one may presume that the Court will give a negative answer (see Case 113/80, *Commission v. Ireland*—"Foreign" for Irish Souvenirs produced abroad not allowed). As to the right of a Member State to reserve specific denominations for specific domestic products,[89] the Court has very rightly decided that an appellation of origin or indication of provenance can only benefit from the protection of Article 36 if there is a link between quality and provenance, and that the definition of the provenance by reference to the national territory could never be justified.[90]

(b) Trade practices and advertising. As long as these matters are not harmonised, Member States largely retain the power to decide what is fair and what is not in relation to advertising and sales promotion on their territory, as long as the rules are indistinctly applicable to domestic and EEC imported products and they are not a disguised protectionist measure. The limits to this jurisdiction and to the implementation and application[91] of these rules have still to be drawn. Imagine the application of advertising rules leading to the prohibition of imports, *e.g.* the prohibition of English or Dutch newspapers or magazines in Belgium because they contain comparative advertisements prohibited under Belgian law: Article 20, 2° Trade Practices Act 1971.

(c) Product regulation. As long as it can reasonably be feared that their abolition could endanger the health of consumers, product security and health regulations are justified under Articles 30–36.

(d) Labelling and product regulation in the future. As far as technical specifications (on quality, safety, quantities, packages, labelling) of products are concerned, attention should be paid to the important Council Directive of March 28, 1983 establishing an

---

[88] For foodstuffs labelling see the provisions of Article 14, Council Directive December 18, 1978, which do not in my opinion *per se* authorise Member States to require that the labelling should always be in the language of the region (as is the case in Article 10 Belgian Royal Decree of October 2, 1980, *Moniteur Belge*, October 11, 1980).

[89] The Commission has brought an action under Article 169 against France and the U.K. (mandatory indication on textiles and some other goods) (Answer of Mr. Nargesto Written Question, O.J., 1983 C 177/19.

[90] Case 12/74, *Commission v. Germany*, [1975] E.C.R. 181: "Sekt" and "Weinbrand" (see criticism of this decision by Beier F.K., "Das Schutzbedürfnis für Herkunftsangaben und Ursprungsverzeichnungen im Gemeinsamen Markt" *GRUR Int.* 1977, p. 1.

[91] Even a Court decision might be a "measure" in the sense of Article 30: Barents, R., n. 24, *ante*, p. 275.

information procedure for technical standards and regulations.[92] Technical standards are non-binding specifications approved by a standards institution. A technical regulation is a technical specification made mandatory by a public authority (see Article 1). The Directive introduces a mandatory notification of all drafts of technical standards and regulations to the Commission. Moreover, a government of a Member State has to suspend for six months the introduction of a new technical regulation, if the Commission or another Member State opposes it within three months of the notification of the draft. If the Commission proposes to harmonise the matter, the period of suspension is even one year. However, this suspension does not apply when a Member State has to work out urgently technical regulations *in relation to public health or safety* (Article 9).

B. Implications for European consumer law and policy.

First it is admitted that the Council and the Commission are in principle as bound by Article 30 as the Member States, but vis-a-vis community institutions such a prohibition has not the same unconditional character in that it is subject to exceptions which are justified on the grounds of the general interest of the Community.[93]

Secondly, European consumer law and policy will necessarily be dependent on the Commission's aims, as expressed in the Communication concerning *Cassis de Dijon*[94] and already put into practice[95] "to tackle a whole body of commercial rules which lay down that products manufactured and marketed in one Member State must fulfil technical or qualitative conditions in order to be admitted to the market of another and specifically in all cases where the trade barriers occasioned by such rules are inadmissible according to the very strict criteria set out by the Court."

An important consequence of the foregoing is: "The Commission will be concentrating (in its work on harmonisation) on sectors deserving priority because of their economic relevance to the creation of a single interval market." In other words, in the area of product regulations consumer protection as such will not be a priority in deciding to approximate the laws. Therefore national product regulations with a lesser relevance for the creation of a common market but of great relevance for the consumer will be tackled before the Court of

---

[92] O.J. 1983 L 109/8 For criticism of the proposals of the directive: Micklitz, H., n. 85 *ante*.
[93] Van Gerven, W., "The recent case law of the Court of Justice concerning Articles 30 and 36 of the E.E.C. Treaty, 1977 C.M.L.R. pp. 2–22; see in detail with nuances: Oliver, P., n. 14, *ante*, pp. 36–42.
[94] O.J. 1980 C 256/2.
[95] See the great number of Article 169 cases pending in relation to national product regulations (*i.e.* Belgian and French law on the mandatory form for margarine packages, the German "Reinheitsgebot" for beer, French caravans, limitation of the use of animal gelatine in Italy . . . and the even greater number of cases pending before the Commission (500 it seems: 22 *BEUC News*, March 1983, p. 2).

Justice, which means that they will either remain or disappear but that a Community regulation is not evisaged. In that context the information procedure of the proposal for a Council Directive cited in the preceding subsection might, if it functions well, develop the important role of providing the Commission with relevant information on all aspects of a problem when it makes its choice between harmonisation (see Article 10, paragraph 2), enforcement action (Article 169) or nothing.

It may be hoped that the Commission when evaluating the priorities from a Common Market point of view will look at the consumer's interest *in* a Common Market. This is a "political" question, including consumers' representation, which is probably more subject to other imponderables than to decisions of principle, such as the *Cassis de Dijon* communication. The case law of the Court does not, in any event, contain one single element which should prevent the Commission and the Council bringing into action its consumer protection programmes of 1975 and 1981.

CONCLUSIONS

Genuine consumer protection has not yet been made impossible by the Court's case law since *Cassis de Dijon* (1979), the case law which in essence is the continuation of the *Dassonville* judgment of 1974.

Consumer interest is *positively* served by these judicial developments in an indirect, and not remote, way: consumers benefit from the breakdown of protectionism.

Nevertheless many other aspects of consumer protection in the area of "social regulation" will only be realised if the European authorities either leave the initiative to the Member States or, better, take appropriate harmonisation or non-legislative steps in spite of, but at the same time because of, *Cassis de Dijon*.

Finally, consumer representatives will probably need to keep a vigilant and careful eye on their governments in case they try to justify their inactivity in the consumer field by referring misleadingly to *Cassis de Dijon*.

APPENDIX

List of cases relating to Articles 30–36 after "Cassis de Dijon"

Case no.	Date	Name	E.C.R.	Matter
1. 147/78	08.04.79	*Ratti*	[1979] 1629	(relation between Arts. 36 and 100)
2. 152/78	10.07.80	Commission v. France	[1980] 2299	(alcohol advertising)
3. 153/78	12.07.79	Commission v. Germany	[1979] 2555	(import of meat)

	Case no.	Date	Name	E.C.R.	Matter
4.	159/78	25.10.79	Commission v. Italy	[1979] 3247	(customs' agents)
5.	177/78	26.06.79	Pigs and Bacon Commission v. McCaren	[1979] 2161	(Art. 34 in relation to common market regulation for meat).
6.	179/78	28.03.79	Rivoira	[1979] 1147	(indication of country of origin in relation to Art. 115)
7.	231/78	29.03.79	Commission v. U.K.	[1979] 1447	(potatoes)
8.	232/78	25.09.79	Commission v. France	[1979] 2729	(import of lamb)
9.	251/78	08.11.79	Denkavit	[1979] 3369	(veterinary checks on animal feed)
10.	5/79	18.10.79	Buys	[1979] 3203	(price freeze)
11.	15/79	08.11.79	Groenveld B.V.	[1979] 3409	(Art. 34 and prohibition on producing horse meat)
12.	16–20/79	06.11.79	Danis	[1979] 3327	(price freeze, notification of price increases)
13.	34/79	14.12.79	Henn and Darby	[1979] 3795	(import restrictions on pornography)
14.	94/79	26.02.80	Vriend	[1980] 327	(mandatory affiliation to official body for marketing of material for plant propagation)
15.	788/79	26.06.80	Gilli & Andres	[1980] 2071	(prohibition of apple vinegar)
16.	823/79	09.10.80	Carciati	[1980] 2773	(taxation of car imports)
17.	27/80	16.12.80	Fietje	[1980] 3839	(labelling liquor)
18.	32/80	28.01.81	Kortmann	[1981] 251	(parallel imports of pharmaceuticals)
19.	53/80	05.02.81	Eyssen	[1981] 409	(nisin)
20.	55 & 57/80	20.01.81	Membran v. Gemma	[1981] 147	(copyright royalties)
21.	58/80	22.01.81	Dansk Supermarket v. Imerco	[1981] 181	(copyright, trade mark and unfair competition)
22.	113/80	17.06.81	Commission v. Ireland	[1981] 1625	(Irish souvenirs)
23.	130/80	19.02.81	Kelderman	[1981] 527	(proportion of dry matter in bread)
24.	132/80	07.04.81	United Foods v. Belgium	[1981] 995	(fish—public health inspection)

Case no.	Date	Name	E.C.R.	Matter
25. 155/80	14.07.81	*Oebel*	[1981] 1993	(prohibition on baking at night, Arts. 30 and 34)
26. 187/80	14.07.81	*Merck* v. *Stephar*	[1981] 2063	(patents on pharmaceuticals)
27. 193/80	09.12.81	*Commission* v. *Italy*	[1981] 3019	(vinegar)
28. 206 seq./80	09.06.82	*Orlandi*	[1982] 2147	(security for import advances)
29. 270/80	09.02.82	*Polydor* v. *Harlequin Record Shops*	[1982] 329	(copyright EEC-Portugal)
30. 272/80	17.12.81	*Biologische Producten*	[1981] 3279	(approval of plant protection products)
31. 1/81	03.12.81	*Pfizer* v. *Eurimpharm*	[1981] 2913	(parallel import of pharmaceuticals and trade marks)
32. 6/81	02.03.82	*Industrie Diensten Groep* v. *Beele*	[1982] 707	(slavish imitation)
33. 75/81	31.03.82	*Blesgen* v. *Belgium*	[1982] 1211	(restrictions on marketing of spirits)
34. 95/81	09.06.82	*Commission* v. *Italy*	[1982] 2187	(security for import advances)
35. 124/81	08.02.83	*Commission* v. *U.K.*	[1982] 203	(U.H.T. milk)
36. 141–143/81	01.04.82	*Holdijk*	[1982] 1299	(Art. 34: protection of fattening calves)
37. 144/81	14.09.82	*Keurkoop* v. *Nancy Kean Gifts*	[1982] 2853	(design protection)
38. 220/81	22.06.82	*Robertson*	[1982] 2349	(hallmarking of silver)
39. 249/81	24.11.82	*Commission* v. *Ireland*	[1982] 4005	("Buy Irish")
40. 261/81	10.11.82	*Rau/De Smedt*	[1982] 3961	(cubical form for margarine)
41. 286/81	15.12.82	*Oosthoek*	[1982] 4575	(prohibition of premium offers)
42. 314–316/81 and 83/83	14.12.82	*Waterkeyn*	[1982] 4337	(interpretation of Case 152/78)
43. 29/82	03.02.83	*Van Luypen*	[1983] 151	(Art. 34: quality control of vegetables)
44. 40/82	15.07.82	*Commission* v. *U.K.*	[1982] 2793	(health import ban for poultry)
45. 42/82	22.03.83	*Commission* v. *France*	[1984] 1013	(import of Italian wine)
46. 59/82	20.04.83	*Schutzverband* v. *Weinvertriebs-GmbH*	[1984] 1217	(alcohol level of vermouth)

	Case no.	Date	Name	E.C.R.	Matter
47.	94/82	17.03.83	*De Kikvorsch*	not yet rep.	(quality standards for beer)
48.	155/82	02.03.83	*Commission* v. *Belgium*	[1983] 531	(licence system for phyto-pharmaceuticals).
49.	172/82	10.03.83	*Fabricants Raffineurs d'huile de graissage* v. *Inter-huiles*	[1983] 555	(prohibition on export of exhaust oil)
50.		22.06.83	*Commission* v. *France*	not yet rep.	(fixed price for imported cigarettes)
51.	174/82	10.07.83	*Sandoz*	not yet rep.	(vitamin additives in foodstuffs)

[1] This list does not contain the cases relating to free movement of goods in which Arts. 30–34 are not raised (*e.g.* a number of judgments on the compatibility of national price regulations with the common organisation of agricultural markets) nor the cases on Arts. 59 *et seq.* (free provision of services).

VII

Consumer Redress Under E.C. Competition Law

Patrick Deboyser[1]

COMPETITION LAW AND THE CONSUMER INTEREST

It has sometimes been suggested that the protection of the consumer interest is the essential, if not sole, object of the EC competition policy. Whilst this is certainly an exaggeration, if only because consumer protection was not a real concern for the EC institutions until the mid–70s, there is little doubt that consumers do indeed benefit from the application of anti-trust law.

Where a breach of competition rules is being committed by manufacturers, importers, wholesalers or distributors, the persons most directly concerned will usually be their competitors, suppliers or customers. However, ultimate users or consumers of the goods in question also suffer either directly as a result of increased costs passed on to them, or indirectly because they are deprived of some of the benefits of competition.

Hence, it is no coincidence that Articles 85 and 86 form one of the only two sections of the Treaty of Rome which go so far as to mention the consumer interest—the other section being, ironically enough, Articles 39 and 40 which set out the objectives and main principles of the Common Agricultural Policy.

Consumers, however, do not benefit from any particular status under EC competition. Remedies available to consumers in case of a breach of EC competition rules are those open to any interested party, *i.e.* any natural or legal person, be it a company or an individual, who claims a legitimate interest.

The purpose of this paper is to review those remedies, by putting special emphasis on problems arising for consumers when exercising their rights under EC competition law.

E.C. COMPETITION LAW AND NATIONAL LAW

The coexistence of two legal orders (the Community and the Member States) raises two different issues. The first one concerns the relationship between Community rules on competition and national law on competition. The second one (dealt with in the next section)

---

[1] Legal Officer, BEUC (Bureau Européen des Unions de Consommateurs)

revolves around the competence for applying whatever rule is to be applied in a given case.

Those questions may look similar to the classical issues of "choice of law" and "jurisdiction" in private international law, but they are not, either in the way the problems arise or in the way they are solved, for the mere reason that Community law and national law are not on an equal footing which is the basic principle of private international law. This is already the clue to the first question: in principle, Community law and national law do not compete; they complement each other. Where they do compete, Community law must however take precedence.

Restrictions on competition which do not affect trade between Member States do not fall within Articles 85 and 86. Such practices will thus be caught only by national competition rules. Restrictions of competition which do affect trade between Member States, in contrast, raise a problem. Indeed, they will restrict competition altogether in at least one Member State. Clearly, the question is whether to apply Community or national competition law.

The authors of the Treaty of Rome were, of course, aware of this problem. Article 87(2)(e) provides that "the relationship between national laws and the provisions contained in this section (Articles 85 and 86) will be determined by regulations or directives adopted by the Council."

As no such regulation or directive has been enacted so far, the relevant principles are those laid down by the European Court of Justice in *Walt Wilhem* v. *Bundeskartellamt*.[2] That case was referred to the European Court in the course of parallel proceedings into the same set of circumstances that were being conducted respectively by the EC Commission and the Bundeskartellamt (the German Federal Cartel Office).

The Court decided that "national authorities may apply their internal laws to agreements, even where the agreement is being examined by the Commission, provided that the application of national law does not prejudice the full and uniform application of Community law or the effect of acts in implementation of it."

As a result, national authorities could not, under national law, accept or authorise an agreement or an abuse of dominant position caught by Articles 85(1) or 86, nor could they condemn under national law an agreement which has been exempted under Article 85(3), either by way of an individual decision or by way of a block exemption.

COMPETENCE FOR APPLYING E.C. COMPETITION LAW

So far, we have resolved potential conflicts between Community competition law and national laws. It remains to be seen which authorities or courts are competent to apply whatever rule is appli-

[2] [1969] E.C.R. 1.

cable. First of all, there could be no doubt as to the application of national competition rules: the Commission and the Court of Justice have no competence whatsoever to put national laws into force. In contrast, national authorities and courts may, indeed have to, apply Community competition rules, since the Treaty and Acts in implementation of it are directly applicable in all Member States.

The competence for the application of Articles 85 and 86 is fixed by Article 9 of Regulation 17, as follows: the Commission has sole power to declare Article 85(1) inapplicable, pursuant to Article 85(3); as long as the Commission has not initiated any proceedings, the authorities of the Member States remain competent to apply Article 85(1) and 86, in accordance with Article 88.

In *B.R.T.* v. *SABAM*[3] the Court of Justice, however, made it clear that national courts, when deciding on civil matters, were not to be regarded as "authorities of the Member States applying Articles 85 and 86 in accordance with Article 88." Thus the authorities meant in Regulation 17 are the administrative bodies in charge of the application of national competition laws, like the German Bundeskartellamt, the French Commission de la Concurrence and the Office of Fair Trading in the United Kingdom.

The Court also held, still in *B.R.T.* v. *SABAM*, that "Articles 85 and 86 produce direct effects in relations between individuals, and consequently create direct rights in respect of the individuals concerned which the national courts must safeguard."

It follows that the direct rights generated by Articles 85 and 86 for individuals must be safeguarded by national courts, notwithstanding the fact that proceedings have been initiated by the EC Commission; and that national courts may, however, for the sake of legal security suspend proceedings until a decision has been reached by the Commission, or ask the Court of Justice for a preliminary ruling according to Article 177.

In practice, however, neither the cumulative application of Community and national competition laws, nor the parallel competence of the EC Commission and national authorities and courts have led to major problems, so that there is little need for a regulation or a directive as provided for in Article 87(2)(e).

APPLYING TO THE E.C. COMMISSION

Under Article 3 of Regulation 17 the Commission may, by a decision, require an undertaking or an association of undertakings to terminate an infringement of Articles 85(1) or 86. Such a decision is thus similar to a "cease and desist" order. The Commission may, in its decision, impose a fine or a periodic penalty.

There are essentially two means by which the Commission may investigate possible infringements of the EC competition rules. First, the Commission has a right of initiative. Secondly, a party to an

---

[3] [1974] E.C.R. 51.

agreement or other persons claiming a legitimate interest may make complaints to the Commission. The Commission must examine the facts submitted in the complaint.

Article 3(2) of Regulation 17 provides that those entitled to make applications are (a) Member States; and (b) natural or legal persons who claim a legitimate interest. There is little doubt that individual consumers as well as consumer organisations fall under this category.

The *Kawasaki*[4] case, for instance, was brought to the attention of the Commission by a Belgian consumer who had tried to import a Kawasaki motorbike from the United Kingdom, where prices were 30 per cent. lower than in Belgium. The Commission subsequently established that Kawasaki Motors (the British importer) had imposed an export ban on its dealer since 1975. The Commission ordered that this ban be lifted, and imposed a fine of £67,000 on the company.

As to the form of the complaint, Regulation 27 provides that any complaint and the supporting documents must be submitted to the Commission with 11 copies. Supporting documents must be either originals or duly certified copies. No particular form is required, although the Commission as a matter of convenience has made available Form C for this purpose.

The Commission also has power to order interim measures (basically similar to an interlocutory injunction) in order to protect the position of a complainant pending the Commission's decision on the complaint. This was, however, a very controversial issue until three years ago. The Commission had indeed always been very reluctant to use this power, and had even issued a statement telling complainants to try national courts first for preservative measures.

In January 1980, the Court of Justice decided in the *Camera Care*[5] case that the Commission has power to order interim measures under the EEC Treaty in competition cases. The Commission had, once more, refused to take interim measures as requested by the Camera Care company. Camera Care appealed to the Court, and the Court found against the Commission. The first, and so far only, case in which the Commission has actually taken interim measures is the *Ford*[6] case. The interim measures had been requested by a consumer organisation (BEUC), but the Commission claimed to act on its own initiative.

CONTROL OVER THE COMMISSION BY THE COURT

The European Court of Justice has four different types of jurisdiction in relation to Articles 85 and 86:

— unlimited jurisdiction to review decisions whereby the Commission has fixed a fine or a periodic penalty;

---

[4] [1979] 1 C.M.L.R. 448.
[5] [1982] 2 C.M.L.R. 233.
[6] [1982] 3 C.M.L.R. 673.

— power to review the legality of formal decisions taken by the Commission (Article 173);
— jurisdiction to declare that the Commission has failed to take action required to be taken by the Treaty (Article 175);
— points of EC competition law appearing in national courts may be referred to the European Court for a preliminary ruling (Article 177).

Moreover, the Court of Justice may in any case before it prescribe interim measures (Article 186).

I said earlier that the Commission "must investigate any facts submitted to it in a formal complaint." In theory, the refusal of the Commission to follow up a case or its failure to investigate it may be appealed to the Court of Justice, respectively under Article 173 and Article 175. This is, however, a difficult issue, as was again demonstrated in *Bethell* v. *Commission*.[7] So far, the Commission has never been condemned by the Court of Justice for its refusal or failure to act in competition cases.

APPLYING TO NATIONAL AUTHORITIES

We have seen earlier that, according to Article 9 of Regulation 17, the authorities of the Member States remain competent to apply Articles 85(1) and 86, as long as the Commission has not initiated proceedings. In doing so, national authorities apply their own rules of procedure. As far as I know, the only national authority to have made use of this power is the Bundeskartellamt (the German Federal Cartel Office).

In the United Kingdom the only authority that has been expressly designated, in the European Community (Designation) Order 1973, is the Secretary of State for Trade. In practice, however, the Director General of Fair Trading is actually acting as a competent authority for various purposes connected with EC competition rules. It is more doubtful whether the Monopolies and Mergers Commission could be regarded as such. In any case, it seems that none of those authorities has any independent power, whether under Regulation 17 or under United Kingdom domestic law, to impose fines or make investigations relating to the enforcement of Articles 85(1) and 86.

The Consumers' Association, publishers of *Which?*, recently submitted evidence of anti-trust practices on the cross-Channel ferry links to the Office of Fair Trading. I understand that they have been advised to refer the matter to the EC Commission, and they are currently preparing with BEUC a formal complaint to the Commission under Article 85.

As was said earlier, as soon as the Commission has actually initiated proceedings, the national authorities are no longer competent to apply Articles 85(1) and 86 to the same facts.

[7] [1982] E.C.R. 2277.

APPLYING TO NATIONAL COURTS

National courts, in contrast, remain competent to apply Articles 85 and 86 in civil matters, notwithstanding the fact that the Commission has initiated proceedings. This was made clear by the European Court of Justice in the above-mentioned *B.R.T.* v. *SABAM* case, in which the Court held that Articles 85 and 86 create direct rights for individuals which national courts must safeguard, subject to Article 177 and the rule in the *Walt Wilhem* v. *Bundeskartellamt* case.

National courts may apply Articles 85 and 86 in

— granting injunctions;
— awarding damages;
— granting declarations by way of relief to a party to a contract;
— permitting reliance on them as a defence to proceedings.

I will comment on only the first two remedies, since neither consumers nor consumer organisations are likely to be concerned with the latter two. The competence of national courts to grant remedies for breach of the EC rules on competition has been a very controversial issue for a long time, and in a way it still is. In 1966 the Commission had a study carried out on the national laws of the then six Member States on this question. The authors concluded that all forms of private remedies were available in all Member States. They expressed certain doubts, however, as to whether Articles 85 and 86 should be regarded as laws for the protection of private interests or merely as laws for the protection of the public interest or the Community.

This is an important question, indeed a decisive one, under both Dutch and German law, where laws for the protection of the public interest do not give rise to a cause of action for individuals. The *B.R.T.* v. *SABAM* case, however, solved that question, when the Court decided that Articles 85 and 86 create direct rights for individuals. Hence, national courts must at least grant the same remedies as they would for a breach of domestic law. Ever since that landmark decision, national courts have granted injunctions for breach of Articles 85 and 86.

In the United Kingdom, Lord Denning held as early as 1974 in *Application des Gaz* v. *Falks Veritas*[8] that Articles 85 and 86 "create new torts."

In 1979 the High Court granted an injunction for breach of Article 85 in *Budgett* v. *British Sugar* (unreported).

THE GARDEN COTTAGE FOODS CASE

Next came the *Garden Cottage Foods* case.[9] Garden Cottage Foods started business in 1980. Most of this business was the purchase and

---
[8] [1974] 2 C.M.L.R. 75.
[9] [1982] 2 C.M.L.R. 542; [1982] Q.B. 1114.

re-sale of bulk butter. Of its purchases between 1980 and 1982, 90 per cent. were from the Milk Marketing Board; and of its re-sales, 95 per cent. were for export to the Netherlands. The Milk Marketing Board is a statutory authority producing some 75 per cent. of the butter produced in England and Wales.

In March 1982, the Milk Marketing Board informed Garden Cottage that it had appointed four independent distributors to handle the sales of its bulk butter for export; Garden Cottage was subsequently advised to contact those distributors to discuss the availability of supplies. Garden Cottage issued a writ alleging contravention of Article 86 and applied for an interlocutory injunction.

Parker J., when faced with the latter application, inevitably decided that there were serious questions to be tried. He next considered whether Garden Cottage would be adequately compensated by an award of damages for loss, if it were to succeed at the trial in establishing that the Milk Marketing Board's refusal to supply it for bulk butter was a contravention of Article 86. He thought so, and thus refused to grant the interlocutory injunction.

The Court of Appeal, however, held that Parker J. was wrong in his view that damages would provide an adequate remedy. Sir Sebag Shaw expressed considerable misgivings as to whether a remedy in damages lies for a contravention of Article 86. Lord Denning M.R. thought there was a good deal to be said for there being a remedy in damages, but it was not altogether certain. May L.J., though less doubtful as to the availability of such a remedy, considered that the contrary was arguable. So the Court allowed the appeal and granted an injunction requiring the Milk Marketing Board to continue supplies to Garden Cottage until the trial.

This decision was in turn appealed to the House of Lords. Lord Diplock said that the Court of Appeal was wrong, and that Parker J. was right and was entitled to take the view that a remedy in damages would be available. Only Lord Wilberforce expressed a different view, because he thought that the Court of Appeal's order made for better justice and he could see nothing wrong with it in law. The House of Lords thus allowed the appeal.

Though the House of Lords' decision[10] is not as clear as one would have hoped, there is little doubt left, in my view, that national courts have to grant injunctions and to award damages (where appropriate) for breaches of Articles 85 and 86.

WHERE TO APPLY?

Neither the Commission nor the Court of Justice have power to award damages to consumers to whom loss is caused by a breach of the EC competition rules. In such cases only national courts may grant compensation.

[10] [1983] 2 All E.R. 770.

The cost of bringing such proceedings, however, will frequently outweigh the possible benefits for individual consumers, since the loss to each consumer caused by a breach of anti-trust law is normally relatively small. The availability of class actions, treble damages and contingent fees would probably change the picture, as the practice with anti-trust complaints in the United States suggests. There is clearly a problem of access to justice. When seeking an injunction, consumers and consumer organisations face an alternative: both the Commission and national courts have powers to grant such an injunction.

In matters of urgency, I would advise complainants to try the national courts. The Commission is very unlikely to deal with an application for interim measures in anything like the time in which an interlocutory injunction would be obtained in a national court. Furthermore, as I mentioned, the Commission is most reluctant to have its time taken up with applications for interim measures.

When there is no such urgency, applying to the Commission offers many advantages. In most cases it will prove to be less expensive than going to court; hiring a lawyer is not necessary, and the application can be made in a mere letter. It is also less hazardous, when the case does not look too good. It is, above all, easier; the complainant can rely on the Commission's power of investigation to substantiate the case; in contrast, the issue of a writ requires the complainant to supply full evidence of the alleged breach. It should be pointed out that discovery procedures are less well developed on the Continent than in the United Kingdom. Finally, injunctions granted by national courts are limited in their territorial scope, whilst the Commission's injunctions are Community-wide.

Summing up, I would suggest that national courts should be tried first for interlocutory injunctions. Otherwise complaining to the Commission is easier. When a decision has been adopted by the Commission (and not annulled by the Court), there is a serious case to be tried for damages in the national courts: the Commission's decision will be regarded as conclusive proof of the infringement and the only problem left will be to substantiate the damage and establish the link with the infringement.

REFERENCES

Temple Lang, "Community Antitrust Law—Compliance and Enforcement," 18 C.M.L.Rev. 1981.
Temple Lang, "The Powers of the Commission to order Interim Measures in Competition Cases," 18 C.M.L.Rev. 1981.
Temple Lang, "Compliance with the Common Market's Antitrust Law," 14 *International Lawyer* 1980.
Temple Lang, "The Position of Third Parties in EEC Competition cases," 3 E.L.Rev. 1978.
Rew, "Action for Damages by Third Parties under English Law for breach of Article 85 EEC," 8 C.M.L.Rev. 1971.

Paines, "Enforcing EEC Competition Law in English Courts," *The Law Society's Gazette*, 1983

Bellamy and Child, *Common Market Law of Competition*, 2nd ed. 1978.

Barounos, Hall and James, *EEC Antitrust Law*, 1975.

VIII

Product Liability—Actual Legislation and Law Reform in Europe

Hans Claudius Taschner[1]

PRODUCT LIABILITY—A PROBLEM OF THE SECOND INDUSTRIAL AGE

The standard of living is rising in all industrial nations. Cars give mobility; aircraft ensure rapid travel; electronic equipment increases productivity; household appliances replace labour. A constantly increasing number of people are enjoying these benefits of modern civilisation. The overwhelming majority of products which make this progress possible are usable and safe. Present production methods, however, cannot (perhaps not yet), in spite of all safety regulations, exclude the possibility that now and then a product is not sufficiently safe or that undetected, perhaps undetectable, defects have crept in. Because we entrust our health and property to these technical products, defects in them may endanger both such legally protected interests. Because the number of people enjoying the benefits of such products is constantly rising, such cases are on the increase.

The problem all industrial nations are facing is to find a fair balance between the following conflicting interests:

—the interest of the user of such products in the greatest possible protection against such damage and in compensation for any unavoidable damage;
—the interest of the producer in keeping to an acceptable level the costs of production in granting such protection and where necessary compensation for damage arising; and
—the general interest in technical progress and increasing productivity while maintaining safety standards.

This is a problem of the second industrial age, one which is typical of all industrial nations and requires a solution. Moreover, the constantly increasing economic interpenetration throughout the world urges a solution, which is as far as possible the same in all States involved in this economic exchange, *i.e.* the approximation of laws on product liability. Product liability is, first of all, a national prob-

---

[1] Head of Division, Directorate General for Internal Market and Industrial Affairs, Commission of the European Communities. The views expressed in this paper are those of the author and are not to be attributed to the Commission of the European Communities.

lem for every industrialised state. Thus, discussions began all over the world, in Scandinavia as well as in Japan, in the United States and in New Zealand, in Australia and in Central Europe. The international organisations have not taken the lead.

It is useful and of real concern to know the present legal situation in most of the Western European states before speaking of national or international law reform.

LEGISLATION IN MOST OF THE MEMBER STATES OF THE COUNCIL OF EUROPE

The Roman Law countries

(1) *France*

The courts have, in a long tradition, developed case law relating to the sale of goods. The "Code Civil" makes a distinction between a seller who knew of a defect and is therefore liable for all damage arising therefrom and one who did not know and is therefore obliged to reimburse only the costs incurred by the purchaser. Since the beginning of the industrial age courts have presumed that the professional seller, whether the producer or the dealer, was aware of the defect and made him liable for all damage resulting therefrom. This has followed from the application of the legal maxim that the professional is obliged to impart his full knowledge to the layman.

The presumption of knowledge of the defect, developed in this way, became irrebuttable in the first few decades of this century. The "leading case" in this respect—this term from an apparently completely different legal sphere is used deliberately in regard to French law also—was significantly a dispute concerning a road accident. The charge that case law in France had completely departed from the Code Civil system was rejected by the Cour de Cassation with a statement which appears astonishing for a codified legal system, but in actual fact is not. The Cour de Cassation stated that it may well be that the authors of the Code Civil had not thought of such cases—new situations would, however, require new legal rules and the courts had the duty and task of adapting the old rules to changed circumstances.

Since that time the legal position in France has been that any producer and any professional dealer of a defective product is obliged, because of an irrebuttable presumption of fault, to compensate for the damage caused by the defect without being able to exclude liability. No financial limitation of liability is permitted. This applies also to the relationship between producer and dealer, *i.e.* in the commercial sector, where the prohibition of a contractual exclusion of liability clause is deeply regretted. Terms like "state of the art defence" or "development risks liability" are unknown in French law.

(2) *Belgium and Luxembourg*

The position is largely the same.

(3) *The Netherlands*

The law has also moved in practice towards a reversal of the burden of proof. The draft of a new sixth Book "Law of obligation" of the "Burgerlijk Wetboek" has recently been adopted by Parliament. Article 6.3.13, which is to lay down legal rules governing product liability through a reversal of the burden of proof, has initially been excluded from the reforms, pending the results of approximation efforts at European level.

(4) *Italy*

Italian law, however, is still based on the classic principle of fault with the traditional distribution of the burden of proof. There are no signs of a change in the direction of consumer protection in this connection, either in case law, legislative reform or public demand.

The German Law Countries

(1) *Germany*

There has been a change in German law in the last few years. The application of the traditional fault principle in product liability law with the burden of proof on the injured plaintiff became the subject of increasing criticism. Wide public interest was aroused in the 1960s due to the thalidomide disaster. In 1968, the 47th German Jurists Conference ("Deutscher Juristentag") discussed the question as to whether the liability of the producer *vis-à-vis* the consumer should be regulated by law or through court decisions and, if so, in what way. The Bundesgerichtshof (Federal High Court) gave a partial answer in the same year by attempting to create at least a partial remedy on the basis of the fault principle through an amendment to procedural law, which is of considerable practical importance. In the "chicken pest" case of November 28, 1968 it relieved a plaintiff of the burden of proof and placed it on the defendant. It is not for the injured party to prove fault on the part of the producer, but for the latter to free himself from the presumption that the defect arose from fault on his part. Since that time the German Supreme Court has tightened up the requirements for discharging such burden, but has stated constantly and expressly that it is the task of the legislator and not the courts to introduce liability irrespective of fault as a general solution to the problem of product liability.

In 1976, the Bundestag adopted with the support of all parties a new Pharmaceuticals Act which lays down under the law relating to liability that the producer of a pharmaceutical product is liable, irrespective of fault, for the injurious effects of that product; however, it limits liability financially to DM 200,000,000 for the total damage and DM 500,000 in individual cases. The law came into force on January 1, 1978.

(2) *Austria*

As well as the German law, Austrian law is based on the principle of fault. But as in the other European states, courts and legal writers felt the same awkwardness towards the solutions reached in applying this principle. For a couple of years the Austrian Supreme Court has tried to help the victims of defective products by procedural means, even if the judges sometimes seem to go beyond the boundaries drawn by the codified law.

(3) *Switzerland*

Quite a similar situation exists in Switzerland. The general clause in the law of torts, Article 41 OR, is conceived on the basis of the fault principle. Courts have developed a system of "Verkehrssicherungspflichten"—"duties to take care in dealing with others." Most legal writers would like to see product liability incorporated in this system. By putting a defective product on the market, the producer has created a risk for the user of this product. For this reason, he is obliged to take every precaution possible to control this situation. If he neglects the necessary and feasable controls, he commits a breach of this duty and is liable. The crucial question remains which control measures are necessary and can be reasonably expected.

The European Common Law countries

(1) *United Kingdom*

One has to distinguish between an action based on the law of sales and an action in tort. In the law of sales there is an implied term (a "condition") by the seller for the "merchantability" of the product sold. If the goods cause damage, the seller is strictly liable. A disclaimer of liability is permitted, but only in commercial relations. Since 1973 it is no longer possible to exclude or limit liability within the relationship between the last seller and the ultimate private buyer, normally the user and the victim. The result that the last seller, the shopkeeper on the corner, bears the damage is socially unsatisfactory.

The tort action is still based on the traditional principle of fault. Since the 1932 case of *Donoghue* v. *Stevenson* and with the more frequent application of the legal rule *res ipsa loquitur* (the circumstances speak for themselves) the person suffering loss or injury finds himself increasingly in a situation in proceedings which approximates to that of presumed fault. In practice, the courts presume negligence to be proven and decide in favour of the final consumer suffering loss or injury.

(2) *Ireland*

The law is the same as in the United Kingdom.

The Scandinavian countries

(1) *Denmark*

The basis of Danish law is the fault principle. Here again the producer has a "duty to take all reasonable care." He will be held liable, if he omits to avoid the risks which may be created by defective products. But courts in this country—a country without codified civil law—allow a great deal of freedom with regard to both

—a presumption of fault on the part of the producer; and
—the distribution of the burden of proof.

There is a clear tendency in the courts' decisions towards a system of strict liability. No court would consider the introduction of such a liability as *ultra vires*, even if done only by case law.

(2) *Sweden*

The same is true in Sweden. Again this law is based—theoretically—on the fault principle. Courts readily take the producer's negligence for granted. There is a new recommendation agreed upon by manufacturers, insurers and consumers to compensate victims who have suffered personal injuries caused by defective pharmaceutical products. A Royal Commission discussed a general solution for the whole domaine of product liability.

(3) *Norway*

The same evolution has taken place. In this country too the courts have established a situation which is equivalent to a system of strict liability.

LAW REFORM

National activities

Before looking at law harmonisation at the wider level, that of the Council of Europe, or at the narrower level, that of the European Communities, attention has to be drawn to national activities. This is to show that the Council of Europe's Convention and the Draft Directive of the European Communities are not at the root of law reform initiatives, as is sometimes thought, and law reform will not be put aside if one or both of those European instruments fail to come into force. Their only aim is to channel these initiatives for the sake of reaching common results.

(1) *United Kingdom*

The thalidomide disaster, which also has its victims in the United Kingdom, led to the setting up of a Royal Commission to examine the whole range of cases of damage hitherto inadequately covered—accidents at work, in the factory and in the home, traffic accidents and accidents with products—where they have caused death or injury, and to propose legislative remedies. At the same time, the Law Commission and the Scottish Law Commission—independent bodies which draw up legal reforms and are responsible only to the Lord Chancellor—are working on the problems of product liability, also with the aim of preparing legislation for the responsible Government departments.

The developments in this Member State of the European Community are all the more significant since on the other side of the world in *New Zealand*, and perhaps in the future in *Australia* also, there is a collectivistic rule on product liability. The close relations between those countries and the United Kingdom should not be overlooked. In New Zealand the victim of a product causing damage receives compensation from the general social insurance system. Such damage is considered to be an accident for which no one is liable. The State has taken on responsibility for a form of compensation—one cannot speak of damages, since the actual loss is not compensated, as only standard fixed payments are made. The State obtains the necessary funds through social insurance contributions. There are no court disputes, nor is there any recourse against the producer. The claim of contributory negligence on the part of the injured party is inadmissible.

In June 1977 the two Law Commissions of the United Kingdom published a common report suggesting the introduction of strict liability for personal injuries, including "development risks," without providing for financial limits. One year later the Royal Commission published its recommendations. As far as traffic accidents are concerned, it proposed a "no fault" scheme like New Zealand. Damage caused by defective products should be compensated according to the Law Commissions' recommendations.

(2) *France*

The Government is going to propose new legislation to codify the law as developed by the courts. On July 21, 1983 the French Parliament adopted a new Act on "consumer protection" which certainly will have some bearing on product liability.

(3) *Germany*

As has been said above, in 1976 Germany introduced a new Pharmaceutical Act dealing with the producer's liability.

European initiatives

The European Communities and the Council of Europe have commenced activity with a view to harmonising the existing laws of their respective Member States with respect to product liability. Harmonisation of law is in fact law reform. Agreement about the rules aimed at replacing national laws can hardly be a compromise solution between the national legislation concerned. It must be the best rule, to a certain extent anticipating new evolution—best in view of the aims for which the European institution has been created.

(1) *The Convention of the Council of Europe*

"To achieve a greater unity between its members is the aim of the Council of Europe," as it has been stated in the introductory remarks of the draft of a "European Convention on Products Liablity in regard to Personal Injury and Death." This unity includes the harmonisation of the different legal systems. The instrument to achieve this goal is the classical means of a Convention based on international public law. By this Convention, "each contracting state shall make its national law conform with the Convention's provisions" (Article 1 § 1 of the Convention). The Convention is "open to signature by the Member States of the Council of Europe" (Article 13 § 1). After three ratifications, it comes into force between the ratifying states (Article 13, § 2 and 3).

Once the Convention has come into force, the Committee of Ministers of the Council of Europe may invite non-member states to accede thereto (Article 14 § 1). As with any other convention of this kind, the Convention may be denounced by any contracting state (Article 18).

At present only four states—Austria, France, Belgium and Luxembourg—have signed the Convention. As far as the three Member States of the European Communities among those states are concerned, no ratification can be expected in the near future, due to their obligations within the European Communities.

(2) *The Draft Directive of the Commission of the European Communities*

Differences between the laws of the Member States in sectors which have a direct effect on the Common Market hinder its development. Therefore, the Treaty establishing the European Economic Community lays down in Article 3 (h) that "the activities of the Community" shall include, in addition to the traditional direct means of establishing such a market mentioned previously, *i.e.* the elimination of customs duties and the establishment of a common customs tariff in respect of third countries, "the approximation of laws of Member States to the extent required for the proper functioning of the common market." In addition, Article 100, a general provision introducing the chapter "Approximation of Laws," lays down that "the Council shall, acting unanimously on a proposal from the Commission, issue directives for the approximation of such provisions laid down by law, regulation or administrative action in Member States as directly affect the establishment or functioning of the common market."

A directive, a Community legal instrument instituted under the Treaty (Article 189 § 3) is a legal order to Member States. It does not, therefore, apply directly to Community citizens in the same way as a regulation (Article 189 § 2). It is binding as to the result to be achieved. The choice of means—law, implementing order, decree—to implement what has been agreed in common is left to Member States. It may therefore be said that a directive is a type of framework law, the details of which are left to Member States.

On July 23, 1976, the Commission unanimously adopted a proposal for a Directive and submitted it to the Council of Ministers. In the Commission's view this proposal represents a possible compromise between the conflicting interests involved and offers an acceptable solution.

The European Parliament and the Economic and Social Committee approved the proposal in 1979 recommending some modifications. The Commission mainly followed those suggestions and submitted a modified draft to the Council of Ministers in September 1979. In January 1980 the Council discussed this revised draft in three readings. In autumn 1981, the working group submitted four basic questions to the Committee of Permanent Representatives. After a long and sometimes difficult deliberation, a compromise has been envisaged which, it is hoped, can be accepted soon by the Member States. Then the Directive can be finalised.

(3) Relationship between the Draft Directive and the Convention

All Member States of the European Communities are Member States of the Council of Europe. Two other members of the latter (Portugal and Spain) have applied for membership of the European Communities. These facts lead to the question how the relationship between the two legal instruments should be viewed. As usual, both European institutions have collaborated closely in the preparation of the respective instruments by exchanging observers who, with the right of intervention, participated in the work of both working groups.

The Convention and Draft Directive are, at least in their present forms, compatible with each other. Compatibility is necessary because the Member States of the European Communities cannot be confronted with incompatible legal instruments. Despite its aim to harmonise the laws of its Member States, the Convention leaves two basic questions open: first, whether or not the strict liability to be introduced should be limited as to amount; and secondly, whether the contracting states may replace the producer's liability by a collective guarantee (Article 12, Convention). Furthermore, the Convention is limited to the compensation of personal injuries, whereas the Directive also provides for liability for damage to property (Article 6). Therefore, the Convention might be considered as a frame within which the Directive should be kept.

THE DRAFT DIRECTIVE AND CONVENTION—A DETAILED ANALYSIS

Who is liable? Who is a producer?

The basic provisions (Article 1 § 1 Directive, and Article 3 § 1 Convention) stipulate a liability of the "producer" of the defective article. This term covers every natural or legal person who is responsible for the production of the article in question. A workman manufactures in a dependant relationship according to the orders of his employer. He is not a producer.

The liability should extend to any producer, whether he has produced the finished article, a component part or the raw material. To avoid misunderstanding it must be said that in the case of components or raw material, these products are defective only to the extent that they render the final product defective. There is no liability of the producer of a non-defective component, even if the finished product is defective.

A channeling of liability to the producer of the product as it appears in the hands of the user would give less protection to the victim, and be unjust in cases where the cause of the defect lies with the producer of the defective component part. If no recourse to the final producer were possible, it would not, contrary to what has been frequently been argued, be less expensive, because the sole liability of the producer of the final product would constitute a "bad risk" for his insurer, since the latter has no means of evaluating the risks presented by the unknown component manufacturers. Insuring a "bad risk" is as expensive as insuring all producers—the final producer and the component manufacturer.

Both texts extend liability to certain categories of persons in the distribution chain who are not producers in the literal sense of this term. There are various reasons for this enlargement of the definition of "producer." Any person who gives the impression of being the producer by putting his name or an equivalent on the article sold shall be liable for its defectiveness (Article 2 § 1 Directive, and Article 3 § 2 Convention). This extension of liability to the dealer is necessary to cover, *e.g.*, large mail order firms which sell, under their own name, goods produced by an unknown producer under precise instructions of the former. An exclusive liability of the real producer would be worthless in these cases.

The same is true, if an anonymous product has caused the damage. Because only the last seller can reveal the identity of his supplier, known only to him, or of the producer, each member of the distribution chain will be exposed to a sort of "vicarious" liability until the identity of the producer has been made known (Article 2 § 2 Directive, and Article 3 § 3 Convention).

Again, the same legal policy governs the provisions holding the importer liable (Article 2 § 3 Directive, and Article 3 § 2 Convention). The victim can hardly be put into the difficult situation of suing a producer under a foreign jurisdiction abroad or attempting to enforce a judgment in his favour there. Due to the fact that the Member States of the European Communities have agreed on a "Convention on Jurisdiction and the Enforcement of Civil and Commercial Judgments," based on Article 220 § 3 EEC Treaty (in force among the six original Member States and coming into force soon between all ten), a direct enforcement of a judgment given in one Member State is possible.

Type of damage

The Directive covers death, personal injuries and damage to property, but not the diminution in value of the defective product itself (Article 6.). The Convention is restricted to compensation for death and personal injuries only (Article 3 § 1).

It is beyond doubt that compensation for personal injury is of primary importance. On the other hand, compensation for damage to property is required within the European Communities because its Council of Ministers invited the Commission in the Community's Consumer Protection Programme of 1975 to make proposals also for the protection of the consumers' economic interests. For this reason, the Commission included damage to property in the Directive, but distinguishes between damage to property in private use—that of the ultimate "consumer" of the product—and in commercial use. Article 6 (b) makes it clear that the new liability system covers all items of property which (1) are objectively destined for private use, and (2) in the actual circumstances of the case subjectively used for this purpose when the damage arose. This distinction leaves on one side all damage to property which has been used in commercial transactions. It should not be overlooked that the aleatoric circumstances of modern mass production are the same in this so-called "commercial sector." The difference lies in the fact that, at least in most of the cases, the partners in those transactions are capable of satisfactorily regulating their respective rights by contractual agreements negotiated on equal terms, so that a fair allocation of the risks involved may be left to them. This is not the case with the relationship of the producer and the ultimate user. On the other hand, to seek protection in those cases by providing for a system of first party insurance would alter the whole tort liability system in most of the European Community Member States.

Kind of liability

(1) *"No fault" liability*

Both European proposals provide for liability disregarding any fault of the producer. This is stated in Article 1 of the Directive by the formulation "whether or not he (the producer) knew or could have known of the defect," while Article 3 § 1 of the Convention states a liability without making references to any notion of fault.

The reason for proposing a liability system disregarding fault is that the concept of fault cannot be adopted as an adequate criterion to solve the problem of distributing the risks which emerge from the circumstances of modern mass production. If—to take the most important category of defects, the "manufacturing defect"—one out of 10,000 items in a production run is inevitably defective and escapes every imaginable control, the producer cannot be blamed for having committed a fault. But to maintain the fault principle would necessarily lead to the result that risks of a fully automated mass production would lie with the user, who would be struck by the inevitable defectiveness of the product as though by an Act of God. Only liability disregarding fault allows one to shift this risk provisionally to the producer—provisionally, because it is not he who must finally bear the consequences in this situation. Normally it will be possible for the producer to include the necessary expenses, *i.e.* the insurance premiums, in the general production expenses which are covered by the market price for the single item. So it is the user himself, or better the "community of all users of the same product line," who in fact pays the price of being compensated in the case of damage caused by a defective product. This economically sound and politically welcome system is only workable on the basis of a liability system disregarding fault.

It depends upon the definition of the term "strict liability," and on the degree of admitting defences, whether this liability may be called "strict liability." To avoid misunderstandings by using preconditioned terms, it is advisable to use exclusively the notion "liability disregarding fault," which can be found in the laws of all Member States of both European institutions.

No distinction has been made with regard to the four categories of defects customarily occurring: manufacturing defects, design defects, instruction defects (lack of warnings) and development risks. All four categories are subject to the same sort of liability. Theoretically, there might be no need to submit each category of defects to the same rigid system. Some of them might perhaps be treated adequately by a liability based on fault if there is, first, a presumption of fault due to a reversal of the onus of proof and, secondly, a tendency to expand the duty to take care. For the sake of a coherent system of product liability it appears desirable not to differentiate between the different categories.

(2) Interaction with existing law

Remaining unaffected are claims with respect to injury or damage which are based on "grounds other than that provided for in this directive," (Article 11 Directive) or "rights . . . according to the ordinary rules of the law of contractual and extra-contractual liability" (Article 12 Convention). The law of sales is particularly relevant. Traditional claims in tort or contract based on fault (or presumption of fault) should not be abolished by the two European instruments. Strict liability may exist side by side with these traditional claims based on fault. The co-existence of two liability systems with different conditions is recognised, and even customary, under many legal systems. The more favourable strict liability system will probably gain acceptance over the more difficult fault claims and those rights whose development is merely historical.

(3) *Limitation of liability?*

The main difference between the Directive and the Convention, which does not make the two texts incompatible, lies in the answer to the question whether or not the proposed strict liability should be limited in amount. The delegations to the Council of Europe could not agree on a common solution. A compromise was reached by agreeing, in principle, on a system of no limitation, but reserving the right of each Contracting state to introduce unilaterally a limitation in its legal system in two ways, globally and per capita. The global limitation, nevertheless, shall "not be less" than the "sum in national currency corresponding to 10 million Special Drawing Rights" (approximately $12.2 million), as defined by the International Monetary Fund, for all damage caused "by identical products having the same defect." The limitation "for each deceased person or person suffering personal injury" shall "not be less" than the sum in national currency corresponding to 70,000 Special Drawing Rights (approximately $85,500).

The Directive proposes a limitation of liability for the whole Community. To leave this question open would, according to the Commission's view, be tantamount to a renunciation of harmonisation of laws on an important, perhaps the most important, point. Article 7 lays down merely an overall limit of 25,000,000 European units of account (EUA) (approximately $32,000,000) for all personal injuries "caused by identical articles having the same defect." The Draft Directive uses the same formulation as the Convention. There is no proposed limit in individual cases. In the case of damage to property, on the contrary, there has been proposed a limitation only in individual cases: 15,000 EUA for damage to movable property (approximately $20,000) and 50,000 EUA for damage to immovable property (approximately $65,000).

The problem of limiting liability is highly controversial, between the different Member States of the European Communities on one side, and between industry and consumer protection organisations on the other. The proponents of such a limitation argue mainly that, if the requirement of fault as a precondition of liability is taken away, this liability would become hazardous for producers. It would be indeterminate and incalculable. Insurance would become extremely expensive, because every imaginable risk would have to be insured. Against the idea of limitation, it has been said, apart from the political plea for increased consumer protection, that the restriction of compensation would lead to injustice; in all those cases the amount available would be smaller than the totality of claims, compensation would only be possible when all claims have been calculated, which could last many years, and the definition of "damage in series," as a precondition of any limitation, is unworkable.

First of all, it should be borne in mind that something like an "unlimited liability" does not exist in practice. Every liability finds its "natural" limitation in the defendant's seizable property, or the company's assets. Every time a claim exceeds these "bases of liability," the person entitled to recover will see his claim decreased. Therefore, the argument must be reduced to the question how far insurance should be sought. If the liability is limited, a limit is placed on the need to insure the risks involved in a product. Risks beyond the limit need not be taken into account. Therefore insurance becomes cheaper. Economically it would not be necessary to insure all imaginable risks and to pay, through the final price of the product, increased premiums.

As far as the objections to limitation are concerned, it is obvious that only the principle of equal apportionment of funds available in "damage in series" can be applied. The maxim of "first come, first served" has to be rejected. The problem lies in the difficulty of determining the total amount of damage, which will only be possible for the category of design defects. If a damage in series with more than 200 victims occurs (the actual limitation would fully cover the damage of this number of victims), such an event will not happen silently and step-by-step. The public will be alerted; the producer will very quickly know of such a medium-size catastrophe. He will immediately be obliged to stop further delivery, to warn all users who have not yet been injured to discontinue use of the defective product, and to recall all defective items. Any failure to carry out these actions will render him liable as a violation of his duty to take care on a fault basis. In these circumstances, it should not be too difficult to determine all loss which has occurred within a reasonable time by public announcements. A partial payment may satisfy all persons already seeking compensation. A retained sum may serve as a reserve for further claims; after a while this may be finally distributed, if no new demands are made.

(4) *Heads of damages*

Article 6 of the Directive defines what should be understood under "damages" within the scope of the basic provision of Article 1. There is, nevertheless, no further definition of the heads of damages, nor will one be found in the Convention. How far compensation goes depends upon the different national laws, which remain unchanged in this respect by both legal instruments which try to harmonise the existing national laws. No codified legal system has a definition of what should be understood by "damage." The award in every individual claim is left to be assessed by the courts. The lack of legal harmony which already exists within one state must be regarded as unavoidable.

Defences

Both proposals allow a series of defences. These defences are:

(1) *It was not the producer who put the defective article into circulation*

Only the voluntary act of putting the article into the stream of commerce actuates the liability of the producer. Any other activity having the same effect but not based on the free decision of the producer, *e.g.* a theft, will not give rise to his liability. (Article 5 Directive, and Article 5 § 1a Convention).

(2) *The product must have been defective when it was put into the stream of commerce*

Any later cause of the defect will naturally not be the responsibility of the producer. This follows from Article 5 Directive and 5 § 1b Convention. Again, this defence is drafted as a rebuttable presumption against the producer that the defect already existed at that decisive moment. This presumption against the producer, with the consequence that no, or insufficient, evidence works against him, is necessary because the victim can hardly produce evidence of whether or not the defect existed at the time the product was put into circulation. The producer is in a better position to prove the contrary.

(3) *Manufactured for economical purposes*

The Convention provides for a third defence, namely that the product must have been *manufactured "for economical purposes"* or *"in the course of the business"* of the producer (Article 5c). Again, this defence is formulated as a presumption that this was the case, but the producer may bring evidence to the contrary. Originally the Directive did not contain such a provision, but did not actually differ in substance. It seemed obvious from the terms used in the basic Article 1 that the liability should only lie with the producer in the course of his business. This derives from the term "producer" which does not include any private activity of manufacturing. For the sake of clarity the Commission modified Article 5 of the Draft Directive to keep it in line with the Convention.

(4) *"Development risks"*

It follows from the system of the Convention that liability for so-called "development risks" is included in this instrument, even though it is not expressly stated in the text as it is in the Directive in Article 1 § 2. Article 5 of the Convention is exhaustive. A defence is not provided to exclude liability for an admitted defect which could not, by any means, be discovered according to the state of scientific and technological development at the time the product was first put into circulation. Some explanation about this term "development risks" is needed. There is a certain misunderstanding due to the fact that English-speaking people in Europe use this term as well as the term "defence of the state of art," both developed and used in the United States but both unknown in Europe.

One should distinguish clearly between the two terms. "*State of the art*" is a notion relevant in determining whether a product was defective or not. The relevant term to define defectiveness is the "safety a person is entitled to expect" (Article 4 Directive, Article 2c Convention). The degree of safety relates to the time when the product was put into circulation. If at that time the *state of the art* was such that no higher degree of safety could have been expected, the product was *not* defective. Consequently, there will be no liability on the producer. Nor will there be any liability, if the safety expectations were tightened up during the time the product was used. The product must have been defective when it was put into circulation. A safe—and therefore not defective—product cannot become defective by the mere fact that an improved product with higher safety expectations was put into circulation by the producer himself. As far as procedure is concerned, it is not a "defence" of the producer but an item for evaluation by the judge.

There are, on the other hand, cases where a product was tested using all tests available and known at the time of production. Even though all means were used, the existing defect—in the sense of lack of safety at that time—was not discovered. The harmful quality was discovered only after the product was used by the public, which is always the best guinea pig. This case can clearly be distinguished from the "state of the art" situation, where the product was not defective. Only in this sense can one speak of a "development risk" liability. This liability is provided for in the Directive, Article 1 § 2, whereas the "state of the art" is an element for evaluation by the judge in finding out whether the product was defective or not. This "time" element is laid down in Article 4 of the Directive.

(5) *Contributory negligence*

The most important defence, namely the victim's own contribution to the damage, is allowed in both drafts. This defence of contributory negligence (in the sense of the law of the United Kingdom, "comparative negligence" in that of American legal parlance) is expressly provided for in Article 4 of the Convention. On the other hand, the Convention reserves expressly the right to each Contracting state to replace Article 4 by a restrictive system limiting the defence of contributory negligence to gross negligence or intentional conduct of the victim. Because contributory negligence is a well-known concept in all Member States of the European Communities, there is normally no reason to incorporate this notion in an instrument trying to harmonise divergent legal systems, as the Directive seeks to do. To mention this defence is normally superfluous. It is self-evident that this defence is open to every defendant producer. To meet some critics from very learned circles, the Commission inserted this defence in the modified version of Article 5.

(6) *Exemption clauses*

The liability of the producer cannot be excluded or limited by any agreement between him and the final user of the defective product. This is said in Article 10 of the Directive or Article 8 of the Convention. To allow contractual modifications would seriously diminish the efficiency of the proposed liability system.

Period of limitation

Time has been used in two respects to mould a producer's liability. Both texts follow the same idea of limiting this liability by proposing a *10 year cut-off period* (Article 9 Directive, and Article 7 Convention). The rationale for this kind of liability limitation is that, on the one hand, technical and scientific knowledge evolves and, on the other hand, expectations as to safety standards of products change within time. The main purpose of these provisions is to counterbalance the inclusion of liability for the so-called "development risks"; only such a time limit justifies the severity of this liability. This purpose also accounts for the length of this cut-off period: 10 years seems to be appropriate to gain experience with new products as dangerous properties are likely to come to light during such a period. A shorter period would not fulfil these requirements. In addition, it may be said that generally medium-term investment products, such as cars or domestic appliances, last for 10 years.

A period of limitation in the correct sense of this term will be found in Article 8 of the Directive and Article 6 of the Convention. Both provisions are materially identical. They restrict the possibility of suing the producer to a period of three years after the three elements of information necessary to bring a claim, namely damage, defect, and identity of the producer, are given to the victim. If a three-year period seems to be too long, it should be kept in mind that both European instruments envisage cases of transnational relationships between plaintiff and defendant which make preparation of claims, or compromises, more time consuming.

IX

Product Liability and Pharmaceuticals in the United Kingdom

Aubrey L. Diamond[1]

No special rules govern liability in the United Kingdom for injuries received from defective pharmaceutical products. The ordinary legal principles apply (apart from the special provisions of the Vaccine Damage Payments Act 1979, dealt with below). But the application of the ordinary rules is affected by the manner pharmaceuticals are distributed and by the special character of such goods and the consequences of their development and use. In this paper the discussion of "product liability" is confined to liability for personal injury or death.

The special character of drugs derives from their inherent capacity to harm. There is no such thing as a safe drug. A distinguished pharmacologist has said that "There is general agreement that drugs prescribed for disease are themselves the cause of a serious amount of disease (adverse reactions), of death, of permanent disability, of recoverable illness and of minor inconvenience."[2] Obviously, most drugs can harm if an overdose is taken. With the amount of drugs currently provided, both on and off prescription, the interaction of two or more different drugs is always a possibility and may be unpleasant. Drugs are given to produce an effect on the patient, but some part of the action of the drug may not be desired—a side effect. A drug may be toxic because of a patient's abnormality, known or unknown, such as the effect of an analgesic on a patient with liver or kidney disease. The idiosyncracies of the individual patient may result in a range of consequences from the failure to give relief to an allergic reaction as extreme as the occasional sudden death attributed to penicillin, one of the safest of antibiotics. Of course, drugs do great good, but that good is inseparable from risk. Generally the risk is worth taking, but it cannot be ignored.

---

[1] Solicitor; Professor of Law in the University of London and Director, Institute of Advanced Legal Studies.
[2] D.R. Laurence and P.N. Bennett *Clinical Pharmacology* (5th ed., 1980), p. 7.

In the ordinary way strict liability for defective goods derives in English law[3] from the terms of a contract. Where goods are sold, the Sale of Goods Act 1979 implies terms relating to the correspondence of the goods with their contractual description, to their quality and to fitness for the purpose for which they are bought.[4] Similar terms are implied in other contracts under which goods are supplied[5] by the Supply of Goods and Services Act 1982.[6] In particular, there will be such implied terms in a contract for work and materials such as a contract by a private patient for professional services coupled with the supply of relevant medicines, for example a contract for immunisation.[7]

A distinction must be drawn at once between private patients and patients receiving drugs under the National Health Service. It is clear that the supply of a drug by a pharmacist in response to the presentation of an N.H.S prescription is not a sale by the pharmacist to the patient even though a prescription charge is made. In *Pfizer Corporation* v. *Ministry of Health*,[8] a case on the powers of a government department under section 46 of the Patents Act 1949, Lord Reid considered the supply of a drug to a hospital outpatient on an N.H.S. prescription which might be dispensed in the hospital dispensary or by an outside pharmacist. He said that in his opinion "there is no sale in this case. Sale is a consensual contract requiring agreement express or implied. In the present case there appears to me to be no need for any agreement. The patient has a statutory right to demand the drug on payment of [the prescription charge]. The hospital has a statutory obligation to supply it on each payment. And if the prescription is presented to a chemist he appears to be bound by his contract with the appropriate authority to supply the drug on receipt of such payment. There is no need for any agreement between the patient and either the hospital or the chemist, and there is certainly no room for bargaining. Moreover the [prescription charge] is not in any true sense the price; the drug may cost

---

[3] Although this paper deals with the law of England and Wales, there is not much material difference between the three legal systems in the United Kingdom in the matters covered by this paper; moreover there is much in common with the law of the Republic of Ireland.

[4] Sale of Goods Act 1979, s.13 (description), s.14(2) (merchantable quality) and s.14(3) (fitness for a particular purpose). This Act applies to Scotland and Northern Ireland as well as to England and Wales.

[5] Pharmaceutical products, as opposed to equipment such as hearing aids or wheelchairs, are unlikely to be supplied on hire-purchase, so we can ignore the Supply of Goods (Implied Terms) Act 1973.

[6] The 1982 Act applies to England and Wales and to Northern Ireland, but not to Scotland.

[7] In *Dodd* v. *Wilson and McWilliam* [1946]2 All E.R. 691, veterinary surgeons were held liable without negligence in respect of defective serum with which they inoculated cattle. See now Supply of Goods and Services Act 1982, s.4(5).

[8] [1965] A.C. 512; [1965] 1 All E.R. 450 (H.L.).

much more and the chemist has a right under his contract with the authority to receive the balance from them. It appears to me that any resemblance between this transaction and a true sale is only superficial."[9]

Where there is a contract for the sale or other supply of goods, the implied terms will apply in the contract between the supplier and the recipient. Where the recipient is a patient, the situation now being considered, no exclusion or variation of the implied terms is possible since the transaction will, it is thought, always be one in which the patient deals "as consumer."[10]

Correspondence with description

The implied term that the goods will correspond with the description is relatively straightforward. The contract for the supply of a drug will always be by description, and if the wrong drug is dispensed (even without any negligence on the pharmacist's part) there will be liability.[11]

Merchantable quality

If the drug supplied is defective as a result of a manufacturing fault or because it has deteriorated,[12] there will be a breach of the implied term of merchantable quality—that the goods "are as fit for the purpose or purposes for which goods of that kind are commonly bought as it is reasonable to expect. . . ." Presumably this term will also be broken where the drug causes unforeseen side effects, as with thalidomide and its effect on the foetus or with clioquinol (sold as Entero-Vioform) and its effect on the nervous system, though it might perhaps be argued that it is not reasonable to expect any drug to be free from unexpected dangers.

Fitness for purpose

Whenever drugs are supplied the pharmacist will know the particular purpose for which they are being obtained insofar as that purpose is for administration to a human being. (He might not know the particular complaint for which the drug is being taken.) There will however be no implied term of fitness for the particular purpose where the circumstances show that it is unreasonable for the patient to rely on the pharmacist's skill or judgment. The pharmacist might call in aid this provision on the ground that his skill or judgment

---

[9] [1965] 1 All E.R. at p. 455. See also Lord Evershed at p. 461, Lord Pearce at p. 463 and Lord Upjohn at p. 466. See also *Appleby* v. *Sleep* [1968] 2 All E.R. 265.
[10] Unfair Contract Terms Act 1977, ss.6, 7 and 12.
[11] *Cf.* the facts of *Kubach* v. *Hollands* [1937] 3 All E.R. 907 where a mixture was supplied instead of a single chemical. (In the third party proceedings in this case s.13 of the Sale of Goods Act does not seem to have been relied upon, or else it may be that the damage was too remote.)
[12] See, *e.g.* Assocation of Public Analysts, Annual Report for 1983, on medicinal products sold by non-pharmacists.

could not be expected to detect a hitherto unknown side effect; the reply to this is that it is irrelevant: for example, the retailer in *Grant* v. *Australian Knitting Mills Ltd.*[13] could not have detected the chemicals in the long underpants. Another, and more persuasive, argument would be that the patient relied exclusively on the doctor's judgment in choosing the appropriate medicine.

TORT

It is unnecessary to dwell at length on possible liability for negligence. The doctor may have prescribed the drug without taking reasonable steps to explore the risk of side effects, reactions with other drugs, or contra-indications. The pharmacist may have dispensed the wrong drug or the wrong strength. The manufacturer may have researched the drug inadequately[14] or there may have been negligence in the manufacturing process. All these possibilities are familiar enough.

As a matter of policy it seems to be generally accepted that a regime of strict liability for defective products is to be preferred to one based on negligence, and the limitations on contractual liability, notably the requirement of privity of contract, have given rise to the proposals for reform of the law put up by the Law Commissions and the Pearson Royal Commission on Civil Liability and Compensation for Personal Injury.[15] For member states of the EEC, the draft Directive concerning Liability for Defective Products dominates the law reform scene.

STATE OF THE ART

The British government has accepted the introduction of a Community regime for strict liability, but has taken the view that the draft Directive does not strike a proper balance between the interests of injured victims and the interests of producers. According to the Minister for Consumer Affairs "one of the most important improvements that we shall be seeking is the incorporation of the 'state of the art' defence."[16]

Exactly what is meant by "state of the art" in this statement is far from clear. In their report "Liability for Defective Products" the Law Commissions rejected a defence "that the product was as safe as the state of the art would allow at the time of production,"[17] but did not elaborate on this phrase. The Royal Commission also

---

[13] [1936] A.C. 85 (P.C.). See also *Frost* v. *Aylesbury Dairy Co.* [1905] 1 K.B. 608, below, and *Randall* v. *Newson* (1877) L.R. 2 Q.B. 102.
[14] *Cf. Vacwell Engineering Co. Ltd.* v. *B.D.H. Chemicals Ltd.* [1969] 3 All E.R. 1681.
[15] Law Com. No. 82, Cmnd. 6831 (1977); Cmnd. 7054 (1978).
[16] Mrs Sally Oppenheim M.P., 991 H.C. Deb. ser.5, col. 1107 (November 4, 1980).
[17] Law Com. No. 82, (1977), paras. 104 and 105. See Peter Cane, "Unsafe Products and the State of the Art: U.K. Proposals" (1979) 3 *Journal Products Liability* 239.

rejected such a defence, which they described in these terms: "There is a further possibility of providing for a special defence for 'development risks.' A dangerous 'design defect' has a greater potential than a 'manufacturing defect' for widespread injuries caused by a single product range. The risks involved particularly affect industries which produce potentially dangerous products, such as chemicals, drugs, aircraft and motor cars, and the more so where these are subject to continuous technological improvements. It is important to such industries to consider whether there should be carried over into a system of strict liability something parallel to the 'state of the art' defence available under the present system of liability in negligence. The production of a new drug is a striking example of the kind of development risk which might be covered by such a defence."[18]

The expression "state of the art" is of American origin, and if one looks at American cases and statutes one sees that there are several different but related ideas brought into a discussion of this defence. They include the following.

Industry standards

The defendant may argue that he is not liable because his practices are in conformity with those adopted by other manufacturers or suppliers in the relevant industry. To speak of "strict liability" and a defence of this nature in the same breath is surely inconsistent. A test of negligence is whether the defendant has taken the care that a reasonably competent member of his trade or business would have taken, and a defence of compliance with industry standards would amount to saying that the liability is for negligence.

Public standards

It is sometimes suggested that strict liability is an acceptable principle but that it should be a defence to have complied with the standards laid down by a public body. Such standards might be of a voluntary nature, where a manufacturer can choose whether or not to comply, as with many of the standards promulgated by the British Standards Institution, or they might be mandatory standards, such as those laid down for crash helmets worn by motorcyclists or for fireguards on electric fires. For example, the Washington Products Liability Act of 1981 provides in section 6.2 that "When the injury-causing aspect of the product was, at the time of manufacture, in compliance with a specific mandatory government contract specification relating to design or warnings, this compliance shall be an absolute defense." A major criticism to be made of such a defence is that it does not take account of the fact that mandatory specifications or standards may get out of date; if new dangers become known, the standards to be expected of manufacturers may rise above those laid down in the public standard. Paradoxically, in

[18] Cmnd. 7054–1, (1978), para. 1258.

such circumstances compliance with mandatory standards would not necessarily be a defence to an action based on negligence.[19]

Highest possible standards

A defence that the defendant's standards are the highest possible may amount to what users of the expression "state of the art" have in mind. In Arizona, for example, the defendant is not liable if he proves that "the plans or designs for the product or the methods and techniques of manufacturing, inspecting, testing and labeling the product conformed with the state of the art at the time the product was first sold by the defendant," and "state of the art" is defined as "the technical, mechanical and scientific knowledge of manufacturing, designing, testing or labeling the same or similar products which was in existence and reasonably feasible for use at the time of manufacture."[20]

This is probably what the Pearson Commission had in mind by "the 'state of the art' defence available under the present system of liability in negligence." It seems clear that compliance with the state of the art in this sense is not, in English law, a defence to the "strict liability" existing under the Sale of Goods Act. In *Frost* v. *Aylesbury Dairy Co.*[21] the plaintiff claimed damages for the death of his wife from typhoid fever caused (as the jury found) by the defendants' milk. The claim was for breach of the implied condition in the contract of sale that the milk was reasonably fit for its purpose, that is, fit for human consumption. The sellers apparently argued that they had taken every possible precaution against infection in the light of scientific knowledge at that time and that since they could not have found out the fault however much skill and judgment they had exercised the buyer could not be said to have relied on their skill or judgment. This argument the court rejected: the implied condition is that the goods are fit for the purpose, not that they are as fit as care and skill can make them.[22]

Development risk

This was seen by the Pearson Commission, in the passage (para. 1258) quoted above, as a narrower defence than "state of the art." It would, it appears, be limited to the risks of the unknown inherent in

---

[19] On a related point, it may be noted that in its evidence to the Pearson Commission the Association of the British Pharmaceutical Industry stated that that industry "does not regard approval of a new product by the Committee on Safety of Medicines as diminishing their own responsibility for it." See Cmnd. 7054–1, para. 1260.
[20] Arizona Revised Statutes, ss.12–681 and 12–683.1.
[21] [1905] 1 K.B. 608 (C.A.).
[22] Compare the controversy before the Supply of Goods and Services Act 1982 as to the implied term of fitness for purpose in contracts of hire.

the development of new products, and is particularly appropriate to the development of new drugs. In recommending that the manufacturer should not be allowed a defence of development risk the Royal Commission observed that "to exclude development risks from a regime of strict liability would be to leave a gap in the compensation cover, through which, for example, the victims of another thalidomide disaster might easily slip" (para. 1259).

AMERICAN LEGISLATION

Fourteen states in the United States have passed legislation relating to product liability dealing with some aspect of what has just been discussed. In some states (Arizona, Indiana, Nebraska and New Hampshire) conformity with the state of the art is a defence.[23] In others (Colorado and Kentucky) it raises a presumption that the product was not defective.[24] Two states have provided a definition, one introducing the concept of feasibility and the other of availability.[25] In other states the term is used without definition but draws some meaning from its context. In Kentucky, for example, it is obviously thought of as being something akin to the standards of the industry (" . . . conformed to the generally recognized and prevailing standards or the state of the art in existence at the time . . . "),[26] while in Colorado the reverse is true (" . . . conformed to the state of the art, as distinguished from industry standards . . . "). In some states the statute creates no defence or presumption but merely provides for the admissibility or inadmissibility of evidence (Arkansas, Idaho and Tennessee).[27] In some states the legislation refers only to conformity with generally prevailing standards (Michigan and Washington),[28] and in others only to governmental standards (Kansas, North Dakota and Utah).[29] In the majority of states, however, there has been no relevant legislation, and (as the passing of legislation suggests) the judicial trend has been to refuse to admit a

---

[23] Arizona Revised Statutes, s.12–683.1, above; Indiana Code 33–1.5, s.4(b) (4); Nebraska, Product Liability Act 1978, s.4; New Hampshire Revised Statutes, s.507–D:4.

[24] Colorado Revised Statutes, s.13–21–403(1); Kentucky, Product Liability Act 1978, s.3(2).

[25] Arizona Revised Statutes, s.12–681.6 (see above). Nebraska, Product Liability Act 1978, s.4: "State of the art as used in this section shall be defined as the best technology reasonably available at the time."

[26] The Indiana Code refers to "the generally recognized state of the art." The Idaho Code, s.6–1306(1), lists "state of the art" with "the custom of the . . . industry or business."

[27] Arkansas, Product Liability Act 1979, s.5 (here, as in some other states, the term "state of the art" is not used but there is a reference to "the state of scientific and technological knowledge"); Idaho Code, s.6–1306(1); Tennessee, Products Liability Act 1978, s.5.

[28] Michigan Compiled Laws, s.2946; Washington, Products Liability Act 1981, s.6.

[29] Kansas, Product Liability Act 1981, s.4; North Dakota, Products Liability Act 1979, s.6.3; Utah Code, s.78–15–6(3).

defence of conforming to the state of the art. "Essentially, state-of-the-art is a negligence defense."[30]

PRODUCING NEW PHARMACEUTICALS

With this background in mind, we can now turn to some of the product liability problems that arise in the production of new pharmaceutical products. The essence of these problems derives from the fact that the effects of a drug cannot be known until it has been widely used by human beings, and sometimes only when many years have elapsed.

After a drug has been developed in the laboratory and studied in relation to its chemical composition and to comparable and similar drugs it will be tested on animals so that some idea of what happens to it in a living body can be gained. At this stage some drugs have to be abandoned because the risk of trying them on human beings would be too great. For those that remain, however, the next stage is to proceed to give them to humans.

Ethics committees

Ethical questions inevitably arise when research involves living beings. The International Code of Medical Ethics says that "Any act or advice which could weaken physical or mental resistance of a human being may be used only in his interest," but the Declaration of Helsinki, adopted by the World Medical Association in 1964 and revised in 1975, recognised that "Medical progress is based on research which ultimately must rest in part on experimentation involving human subjects."

Neither the medical researcher carrying out the research nor a pharmaceutical company sponsoring it is disinterested in judging the ethical issues, and a "basic principle" in the Declaration of Helsinki is that "The design and performance of each experimental procedure involving human subjects should be clearly formulated in an experimental protocol which should be transmitted to a specially appointed independent committee for consideration, comment and guidance" (para. I.2).

In 1967 the Royal College of Physicians published a report, "Supervision of the Ethics of Clinical Investigation in Institutions," which advocated independent ethical review of research. Since then ethics committees have been set up by most teaching hospitals and by many health authorities, though consideration of research protocols by ethics committees is not at present legally mandatory. Although most members of ethics committees are medically qualified, members of related professions, such as nurses, are often

---

[30] *Beshada* v. *Johns-Manville Products Corp.* 447 A.2d 539, 546 (Sup. Ct. of New Jersey, 1982).

included and some committees have one or two lay members (including lawyers). The "Proposed International Guidelines for Biomedical Research involving Human Subjects" published for discussion in 1982 by WHO and the Council for International Organizations of Medical Sciences lays down a principle that ethical review committees may "with advantage, accommodate respected lay opinion in a manner that provides effective representation of community as well as medical interests."[31]

Trials on healthy volunteers

Although drugs are developed to help the sick, they must be tried on healthy persons first. These voluntary guinea pigs are known as "healthy volunteers." They are volunteers in the sense that they volunteer, but they may well be paid for the time and inconvenience, particularly if they are students.

Whether or not they are paid, the healthy volunteers do not pay for the drugs and it is manifest that there is no contract for the supply of goods to them and hence no implied terms from which they can benefit. Prima facie, therefore, in the present state of English law any remedy, if a volunteer suffered injury from the drug, would depend on negligence. Since negligence, though possible, is rare and likely to be hard to prove, the chances of entitlement to compensation would be slight.

In June 1970 the Association of the British Pharmaceutical Industry (ABPI) recommended to its members that a draft form of contract, proposed in "The report of the committee to investigate medical experiments on staff volunteers" (ABPI, undated), should be used where members of the company's own staff volunteered to take part in experiments. The view is now taken that this recommendation should also apply to other healthy volunteers. The form is set out in Appendix 1 to this paper. It will be seen that clause 4 provides for compensation "without regard to the question of legal liability." This is, I think, what we mean by "strict liability." All that is needed to secure compensation is to establish causation: no fault need be established.

All credit must be given to ABPI for recognising the injustice of liability based on negligence as long ago as 1970, but a major criticism of the draft form of contract must be that, apparently, the burden of proving causation is on the volunteer. If, after the drug has been administered, an adverse condition is diagnosed, the pharmaceutical company may be able to offer an explanation how this might have happened to a formerly healthy person, but if they can-

---

[31] On ethics committees see, *inter alia*, M.J. Denham, A. Foster and D.A.J. Tyrell, "Work of a district ethical committee," *British Medical Journal* 1979, ii: 1042; I.E. Thompson *et al.* "Research ethical committees in Scotland," *British Medical Journal* 1981, 282: 718; Ethical Committee, UCH, "Experience at a clinical research ethical review committee," *British Medical Journal* 1982, 283: 1312.

not do so it would seem to be appropriate to attribute the condition to the drug. Otherwise the volunteer is faced with a problem of proof that may be insuperable, as we will see later on.

It is true that there is an arbitration clause, and that this, by referring to an arbitrator appointed by the President of one of the medical colleges, envisages a medical arbitrator. A doctor may not be as technical on evidential matters as a judge. Nevertheless, when the drug reaction mimics a condition that occasionally occurs spontaneously, even a non-technical arbitrator may well reject a claim if proof lies on the claimant.

Another defect in the contract is that no indication is given as to how "appropriate" compensation is to be fixed. Here, the arbitrator's power to consult a barrister as to the amount of compensation suggests that the compensation is to be related to awards of damages in the courts for comparable injuries. Since the function of damages is to compensate, it is difficult to see any other basis on which the amount of compensation might be arrived at.

Clinical trials

Before a product licence can be granted the drug must undergo clinical trials, trials on persons suffering from the complaint for which the drug is to be made available, under section 31 of the Medicines Act 1968. The Department of Health and Social Security issues a Clinical Trial Certificate after submission of full laboratory data, but there is the simpler alternative of submitting summaries with a confirmation from the medical adviser to the company that he is satisfied that it is reasonable for the trial to take place. Then the DHSS has a maximum of nine weeks (more usually five weeks) to object.[32] Clinical trials are usually conducted in three different centres, at each under the supervision of a named investigator.

Local ethics committees, before giving approval to such trials, have for some time expressed concern at the risk undertaken by patients in this stage of research. As a matter of statistics, the risk is slight. But for any individual patient the consequences could, of course, be serious. Medical advances are in the interests of the whole community, and the individual patient may well benefit from the new treatment, but some ethics committees sought assurances that should a patient be adversely affected, compensation would be forthcoming. As with healthy volunteers, the prospects for a claim based on negligence would be poor.

After some resistance at first, a growing number of pharmaceutical companies recognised that the validity of the case for compensation for patient volunteers was comparable to that for healthy volunteers, and in August 1983 ABPI issued to its members guide-

---

[32] See the Medicines (Exemptions from Licences) (Clinical Trials) Order 1981 (S.I. 1981 No. 164).

lines accepting the principle of compensation. These are set out in Appendix 2 to this paper.[33]

A striking difference from the position of healthy volunteers emerges at once. It is not envisaged that each patient volunteer should enter into a contract with the pharmaceutical company sponsoring the trial and, indeed, the recommendation is for acceptance of the guidelines "without legal commitment." That there could not be a legal commitment without a contract is evident, and though there might be a contract between the pharmaceutical company and the investigating institution or leading researcher, such a contract, though for the benefit of individual patients, would present difficulties of enforcement in English law because of the doctrine of privity of contract. Separate contracts with each patient, though theoretically possible, would not be welcomed by medical staff nor, it must be admitted, by some pharmaceutical companies, so the inclusion of such a requirement in the guidelines might have imperilled their acceptance at all.

Short of a legal commitment, guideline (a) does say that the company should *favourably* consider the provision of compensation, though guideline (b) requires causation on a balance of probabilities. An ambiguity may be noted in this regard. The draft contract for healthy volunteers provides for compensation for any deterioration in health "caused by my participation in the" trial. The introduction to the patient-volunteer guidelines talks of compensation "should they be adversely affected by reason of their involvement in the trial." But guideline (b) talks of injury "attributable to the company's medicine under trial." Here there is uncertainty. Would compensation be payable if the injury occurred as a result of the investigative procedures necessitated by the trial, as for example the insertion of a catheter into a patient's heart by way of a vein? Injury could occur without any negligence by the medical practitioner, and so would not be excluded by guideline (f)(ii). If the procedure would not have been undertaken but for the trial, compensation ought in fairness to be payable. Guideline (b) seems to limit the company's moral obligation to injury caused by the medicine, though it could perhaps be understood as referring to "the medicine under trial" in the sense of the medicine being under trial. (Guideline (g) does not include any element of causation.)

How would such an ambiguity be resolved? Since there is no contract an arbitration clause in the traditional sense is inappropriate, but I.C.I.'s experience in relation to the Practolol tragedy suggests that it would have been wise to provide for independent opinions on the application of the guidelines, typically by a combination of a doctor and a lawyer. In the absence of appointments of independent

---

[33] Strict liability was also proposed in the consultation paper, "Proposed International Guidelines for Biomedical Research involving Human Subjects," a joint project of WHO and the Council for International Organizations of Medical Sciences, 1982, paras. 30–32.

experts by a company—or, preferably, by the President of one of the Royal Colleges—once a dispute has arisen, the guidelines may be treated as leaving all disputed questions to the discretion of the company itself, a procedure unlikely to allay suspicions if the discretion is exercised in the company's favour. (The introduction does use the phrase "by a simple procedure," but no procedure is laid down.)

As to the amount of compensation, again the key word is "appropriate"; "appropriate to the nature, severity and persistence of the injury" (guideline (j)). There is, however, provision for abatement, or even exclusion, of the compensation in the light of six factors listed in three paragraphs. An "extreme example" is given, based on a severe disease, in the advanced stages of which all existing drugs have serious and common side-effects and at the same time poor or uncertain therapeutic value. It seems reasonable that patients trying a new drug as a last resort, when all else has failed, should not be entitled to compensation for side-effects no worse than those risked with any other treatment. It would however be unfortunate if drug companies sought to apply the abatement provision without independent advice, for the charge of seeking to be judges in their own cause could counteract any credit they might otherwise obtain for adopting the guiding principle of compensation.

Product licence

After satisfactory completion of clinical trials, the Minister issues a product licence under section 7 of the Medicines Act 1968 which permits the advertising and marketing of the drug. Product licences are normally valid for five years.

Post-marketing surveillance

Only after the product licence has been granted does really large-scale testing occur on a significant proportion of the population, and post-marketing surveillance ought therefore to be regarded as an important part of the trials given to drugs. The Committee on Safety of Medicines issues free to medical practitioners the "yellow cards" on which suspected adverse reactions may be reported. More than 10,000 cards are returned every year, but some important reactions have first come to light on publication in learned journals, as occurred with practolol (Eraldin) and benoxaprofen (Opren). Practitioners' attention is particularly drawn to the need to report all suspected reactions to recently introduced drugs, marked with a symbol in the British National Formulary, the Monthly Index of Medical Specialities, and the data sheets that must be prepared and circulated by manufacturers.

The General Medical Council published a new edition of its pamphlet *Professional Conduct and Discipline: Fitness to Practise* in August 1983. This contained a new section on "Relationships between the medical profession and the pharmaceutical and allied industries" which for the first time gave guidance on the practice sometimes adopted whereby doctors are offered payment for reporting reactions: "It may be improper for a doctor to accept per capita or other payments under arrangements for recording clinical assessments of a licensed medicinal product, whereby he is asked to report reactions which he has observed in patients for whom he has prescribed the drug, unless the payments have been approved by a relevant national or local ethical committee. It is improper for a doctor to accept payment in money or kind which could influence his professional assessment of the therapeutic value of a new drug."

CAUSATION

A problem that underlies all provisions for compensation for drug-induced injuries is that of proving causation. The adverse effect may follow the taking of a drug, but was it *caused* by the drug? Was the drug the only drug taken by the patient in a relevant period? (And what period is relevant?) Has there been sufficient experience of the new drug for medical opinion to have evolved?

Although statistical evidence may be inadmissible as hearsay,[34] the opinion of experts based on statistics prepared by others is nevertheless admissible.[35] It is also clear that expert witnesses may refer to publications by others so that those publications are in a sense admissible in their own right.[36]

Even if causation by the drug alleged can be proved, that may not implicate any particular manufacturer. Doctors are encouraged by DHSS to prescribe drugs of a type manufactured by two or more manufacturers by reference to their non-proprietary names rather than under the proprietary name adopted by a particular manufacturer—"generic prescribing"—and even if records are kept showing the drug dispensed on a specific occasion, over a period of time a patient may take the same drug as produced by different manufacturers.

A NO-FAULT SCHEME?

Enough has been said to show that negligence as a basis of liability for drug-induced injury is not satisfactory, as has been recognised by the pharmaceutical industry itself in its healthy volunteer contract and its guidelines in relation to clinical trials. The dividing line between clinical trials and marketing after a product licence has been issued may be an important one for the industry but lacks substance as far as an innocent victim of an unforeseen side effect is concerned. After the issue of a product licence, however, the State is

---

[34] *Cf. Myers* v. *D.P.P.* [1965] A.C. 1001 (H.L.).
[35] *R.* v. *Abadom* [1983] 1 All E.R. 364 (C.A.).
[36] *Seyfang* v. *G.D. Searle & Co.* [1973] Q.B. 148, 151 *per* Cooke J.; *H.* v. *Schering Chemicals Ltd.* [1983] 1 All E.R. 849, *per* Bingham J. (on which see also *Schering Chemicals Ltd.* v. *Falkman Ltd.* [1981] 2 All E.R. 321).

necessarily involved, both because the licensing authority is a Minister and because the National Health Service is the largest disseminator of drugs.

In Sweden a no-fault[37] scheme in respect of drug-induced injuries has been introduced. In West Germany, on the other hand, manufacturers are under strict liability. In the United Kingdom there is a no-fault scheme in force in respect of vaccine-caused injury for specific diseases under the Vaccine Damage Payments Act 1979, the first of the Pearson Commission recommendations to be implemented. The Pearson Commission did not recommend a no-fault scheme for medical accidents generally, partly because of the difficulty of establishing causation (paras. 1364–1371). Such a scheme for drug injuries was not rejected by the Law Commission and was rather favoured by the Scottish Law Commission. It is the only solution for the drug injury problem that would deal with generic prescribing.

---

[37] "No-fault" is used here in the same sense as in the Pearson Report: "We use it to refer to compensation which is obtainable without proving fault and is provided outside the tort system. No-fault compensation is a system of obtaining payment from a fund instead of proceeding against the person responsible for the injury." Cmnd. 7054–1, para. 34.

APPENDIX 1[1]

Draft form of contract

Volunteer contract

1 I, the undersigned voluntarily agree to take part in ....

2 I have been given a full explanation of the purpose of the experiment/trial/test and what I will be expected to do (and Dr .... has told me about any possible ill-effects on my health or well-being that might result).

3 I agree to co-operate faithfully with the supervising Doctor and will tell him at once if I suffer any unexpected and unusual symptoms.

4 I understand that in the event of my suffering any deterioration in health or well-being or any harmful susceptibility or toxicity caused by my participation in the experiment/trial/test I will receive appropriate compensation without regard to the question of legal liability.

5 I agree that any dispute or difference as to the application of clause 4 shall be referred to an arbitrator appointed by the President of the Royal College of .... of .... with power in the arbitrator to consult a barrister of 10 years standing with regard to the amount of compensation.

Signed ....

Dated ....

Signed ....

on behalf of ....
(the Manufacturer)

Dated ....

---

[1] Permission to reproduce the documents in Appendices 1 and 2, granted by the Association of the British Pharmaceutical Industry, is gratefully acknowledged.

APPENDIX 2
Guidelines

Clinical trials – compensation for medicine-induced injury

It is becoming common practice for ethical committees to expect assurance that patients participating in clinical trials will be appropriately compensated, by a simple procedure, should they be adversely affected by reason of their involvement in the trial. While such adverse effects are very uncommon, the Association of the British Pharmaceutical Industry (ABPI) accepts this as a guiding principle and has noted that quite different considerations apply to medicines undergoing clinical trial compared to medicines generally available on prescription. Consequently, in cases where injury is attributable to a medicine in clinical trial, the ABPI recommends to its member companies that the following guidelines should be accepted without legal commitment on the part of the member companies:

(a) The company should favourably consider the provision of compensation for personal injury, including death, in accordance with these guidelines but without the requirement for negligence to be proved against the company.

(b) Compensation should only be paid when there is a balance of probabilities that the injury (including exacerbation of an existing condition) was attributable to the company's medicine under trial.

(c) Compensation should only be paid for the more serious injury of an enduring and disabling character, and not for temporary pain or discomfort or less serious or curable complaints such as skin rashes.

(d) These guidelines only apply to injuries to patients involved in clinical trials, conventionally known as Phase II or Phase III trials, that is to say, patients under treatment and surveillance (usually in hospital) and suffering from the ailment which the medicine under trial is intended to treat. These guidelines do not apply to injuries arising from studies on healthy volunteers (Phase I), whether or not they are in hospital, for which separate guidelines for compensation already exist. These guidelines also do not apply to injuries arising from clinical trials on marketed products, except when the trial is on a marketed medicinal product being tested for a prospective indication not yet authorised by inclusion in a product licence.

(e) These guidelines apply to an injury whether or not the adverse reaction causing the injury was foreseeable or predictable although compensation may be abated or excluded in the light of the factors mentioned in paragraph (j) below.

(f) Compensation should not be payable (or should be abated, as the case may be) (i) when there has been a significant departure from the agreed protocol, (ii) where the injury was attributable to the wrongful act or default of a third party, including a doctor's failure to deal adequately with an adverse reaction, or (iii) when there has been contributory negligence by a patient.

(g) Compensation should only be payable to patients receiving the medicine under trial and, therefore, not to control patients not receiving the trial medicine nor to patients receiving placebos, nor to patients receiving other non-trial drugs or medicines for the purpose of comparison with the medicine under trial.

(h) The giving of consents to participate in a clinical trial, whether in writing or otherwise, should not exclude a patient from the benefits of compensation or in any way prejudice his position under the guidelines, although compensation may be abated or excluded in the light of the factors mentioned in paragraph (j) below.

(i) No compensation should be paid for the failure of a medicine to have its intended effect or to provide any other benefit to the patient. This includes the failure of any vaccine or other preparation to provide the preventive or prophylactic effect for which it is under trial, and the failure of any contraceptive preparation or device to prevent pregnancy.

(j) The amount of any compensation paid by the company should be appropriate to the nature, severity and persistence of the injury. However such compensation may be abated, or in certain circumstances excluded, in the light of the following factors (on which will depend the kind of risk the patient should be expected to accept):—

  (i) the seriousness of the disease being treated, the degree of probability that adverse reactions will occur and any warnings given;
  (ii) the hazards of established treatments relative to those known or suspected of the trial medicine, and
  (iii) the availability and relative efficacy of alternative treatments that the patient could have had if he had not volunteered for the trial.

Note This guideline assumes that the level of any compensation paid will depend upon the circumstances in the light of the factors mentioned above. As an extreme example, there may be a patient suffering from serious or mortal disease such as cancer who is warned of a certain defined risk of adverse reaction. Participation in the trial is then based on an expectation that the benefit/risk ratio associated with participation is better than that associated with alternative treatment. It is, therefore, reasonable that the patient accepts the high risk and should not expect compensation for the occurrence of the adverse reaction of which he or she was told.

The Association of the British Pharmaceutical Industry
© Copyright August 1983

Index

Advertising
  abuses, 46
  administrative control, 50
  alcoholic drinks, 42, 43
  Bargain Offers Orders, 57
  British Codes, 61
  class actions, 49
  comparative, 41
  consumer law, 97
  consumer protection, 39
  corrective measures, 48
  cross frontier, 42
  Court of Justice, approach of, 42
  EEC Directive (proposed), 44
    remedies provided in, 47
  European approaches, 41
  harmonisation policy of, 40, 51
  legal controls, 59
  legal enforcement systems, 66
  media associations, 61
  member states
    different rules in, 42
  misleading and unfair, 39 *et seq.*
  misleading and unfair
    EEC Consumer Programme, 39
    effects of, 44
  offensive, 62
  passing-off, 49
  pharmaceutical products, 72, 73
  prohibition on, 42
  prosecution, rates of, 62
  public responsibility, 51
  quantitative restrictions, 42
  remedies, 47
  satellite, by, 44
  self-regulation in, 53 *et seq.*
  self-regulation
    enforcement, 59
    fairness of, 66
    harmonisation policy, 58
    inadequacies, 60
    legislation, 57
    limitations, 58
    political acceptability, 67

Advertising—*cont.*
  socialist countries, 67
  system, 60
  standards, 44
  surveys, 63 *et seq.*
  tobacco, 72
  trademarks, 41, 46
  unfair competition, 39–41
  Advertising Standards Authority, 53
  survey evidence, 65
Agricultural products
  consumer protection, 31
  prices, 31
Air pollution
  Directives on, 37
America
  product liability, 135
Association of British
  Pharmaceutical Industry, 137
Austria
  product liability, 116

Belgium
  product liability, 114
BEUC, 33, 35, 106, 107
  survey, 63
Biologische Producten Case, 28
Blesgen Case, 83, 84

Camera Case, 106
Cassis de Dijon Case, 13, 15, 27, 43, 77, 80–85, 98
CEN, 30
CENELEC, 30
Clinical trials, 138
  compensation, 140
  contracts, 139
  volunteers, 139
  "yellow cards," 140
Code of Advertising Practice
  Committee, 60
Commercial transactions
  fairness, 90
Commission
  competition rules, 105

147

Committee on Safety of Medicines, 140
Common Agricultural Policy, 103
Common Market
  consumer interest in, 99
  consumer protection, 5, 6, 11 *et seq.*
  distortion of competition, 3
  harmonisation policy, 3
Community action
  consumer protection, 9
Comparative advertising
  consumer interests, 46
  EEC Directive, proposed, 45
Compensation and product liability
  causation, problem of, 141
  clinical trials, 145–146
  pharmaceutical products, 140
Competition
  enterprises, between, 8
Competition law
  application of, 104–105
  "cease and desist," 105
  Commission, application to, 105
  complaint, form of, 106
  damages, 109
  Garden Cottage Foods Case, 108
  individuals' rights, 105, 108
  infringement, 105
  institutions, role of, 105
  interim measures, 106
  national authorities, role of, 107
  national law, relationship with, 103, 108
  Regulation 17, 105–106
  remedies in national courts, 108
Competition policy
  advertising, 42
  consumer protection, 103
  Messina Report, 7
  price fixing, 32
  remedies, 103
Conflicting interests
  industrial nations, between, 113
Consumers' Association, 61, 107
Consumer credit
  Consumer Credit Act 1974, 33
  harmonisation, 20
Consumer information
  dangerous products, 35
  energy consumption, 36
  labelling, 35
  origin markings, 36

Consumer information—*cont.*
  pharmaceutical industry, 35
Consumer interest
  definition of, 79
Consumer law
  advertising, 97
  Community policy, 98
  Directive, 94
  European, 98
  future, 97
  harmonisation, 94
  labelling, 96
  national and European, 93
  policy, 93, 95
  product regulation, 97
  trade practices, 97
Consumer organisations, 26, 33
  European, 30
Consumer policy
  basic rights, 27
  Court of Justice, 94
  EEC Treaty, 25, 26
Consumer protection, 1–23, 25, 82, 91, 92
  activist policy, 10
  advertising, 39, 59
  advertising
    self-regulation, 53
  agricultural policy, 31
  barriers, elimination of, 4
  basic rights, 27
  Cassis de Dijon Case, 93, 95
  chemicals, 29
  Commission, 4, 7, 17
  Common Market, 5, 11 *et seq.*
  common standards
    testing, in, 15
  Community powers, 4, 9, 10
  Competition
    distortion of, 3, 5, 7
  competition policy, 32, 103
  comparative advertising, 46
  Consumers' Consultative
    Committee 1973, 18
  consumer organisations, influence of, 26
  consumer, role of, 17, 79
  contract, standard terms, 17
  cosmetics, 29, 36
  Council Resolution 1975, 18
  credit facilities, 33
  cross-frontier effects, 16

Consumer protection—*cont.*
  damages, 109
  dangerous products, 30
  Danish Report, 2
  defective products, 18, 19
    proposed Directive, 18, 19
  discriminatory measures, effect of, 87
  doorstep contracts, 73
    proposed Directive, 19
  duty-free imports, 34
  economic interests, 33
  EEC, competence of, 69
  EEC Report, 5
  electrical goods, 29, 30
  European, 25
    progress report, 25 *et seq.*
  free movement of goods, 77
  general, 1, 16, 22, 23
  harmonisation, 26
    consumer credit, 20
    foodstuffs, prices of, 21
    labelling, selling, foodstuffs, 20
    national measures, 6
    unfair advertising, 19
  health and safety, 21, 27 *et seq.*, 88
  home study courses, 19
  inactivist policy, 10
  industrial property, 87
  information, 35
  insurance, 33 *et seq.*
  integration, policy of, 78
  interest groups, various, 25
  international Conventions, 37
  judicial development, 99
  labelling, 93
  legal basis of, 1, 9
  licensing system, 28
  marketing practices, 70
  measures, 18 *et seq.*
  Member State, action of, 10
  Member State competence, 27
  Messina Report, 3
  motor vehicles, 28
  national measures, 92
    direct effect on, 6
  non-legislative, 96
  packaging, 28
  pesticides, 28
  pharmaceutical products, 28, 30
  policy, 1, 2, 5, 9, 26
    harmonisation, 2

Consumer protection—*cont.*
  policy—*cont.*
    liberal approach, 4
    restrictive approach, 2
    political considerations, 11
    Preliminary Programme, the, 7
  premium offers, 71
  prices, fixing of, 31 *et seq.*
  principle of equivalence, 92
  procedure, 29
  product liability, 124
  product safety, 26, 27
  products, standardisation of, 30, 31
  Programme, 1
  proposals, 18 *et seq.*
  public health, 88
  safety, 95
  satellite television, 72
  scientific committees, 27
  services, 34
  symbols, 36
  tourists, 34
  toys, 29
  trademark law, 37
  unfair advertising, 7
  unfair contract terms, 74
  vitamins, 28
Contract
  implied terms, 130
  unfair terms, 74
Contributory negligence
  product liability, 127
Corrective advertisements, 48
Cosmetics
  consumer information, 36
Council of Europe, 114
  Convention of, 119, 120
  product liability, 121–128
Council Resolution
  consumer protection, 18

Damages
  competition law, breach of, 109
  national laws, 125
  product liability, 122, 125
Dangerous products, 133
  consumer information, 36
Danish Report, 2
Dassonville Case, 81, 99
Death
  product liability, 129

Free movement of goods—*cont.*
  health controls, 87
  indistinctly applicable measures, 83
  industrial property, protection of, 87
  measures of equivalent effect, 81
  national laws, relation between, 81
  national measures challenged, 86
  price control, 90
  principle of equivalence, 92
  product origin, 83
  proportionality principle, 84
  protectionism, 87
  public health, 81
  public policy exception, 86
  "rule of reason," 85, 89
  "trade rules," 84

Garden Cottage Foods Case, 108
General Medical Council, 140
Germany
  product liability, 115, 118

Harmonisation
  Cassis de Dijon Case, 13, 15
  consumer credit
    proposed Directive, 20
  consumer law, 94
  consumer protection
    Commission policy, 22
    Council policy, 22
    EEC, role of, 11
    European Court of Justice, 13
    legislation, 15
    measures, 18 *et seq.*
    Member State, role of, 11
  currency, 8
  free movement of goods, 77
  marketing practices, 70
  Messina Report, 7 *et seq.*
  negative, 13
  product liability, 113, 117, 120
  unfair competition, 91
  unfair contract terms, 74
Health and Safety, 27
  consumer protection, 26
  harmonisation, rules on, 21
  marketing practices, 69
Health controls
  free movement of goods, 86, 87

Hoffman–La Roche Case, 32

Individuals' rights
  competition policy, 108
Industrial property rights, 40
  advertising, 49
  passing-off, 49
Industry standards
  pharmaceutical products, 133
Injunctions
  competition law, 110
Injury
  drug-induced, 141
INNO Case, 32
Insurance services
  consumer protection, 33, 34
Interim measures
  competition law, 106
  Court of Justice, 107
International Monetary Fund
  product liability, 124
Ireland
  product liability, 116
Italy
  product liability, 115

Labelling
  consumer law, 97
Law reform
  public liability, 113, 117
Limitation period
  product liability, 128
Limited liability
  products, 124
Luxembourg
  product liability, 114

Marketing practices, 69 *et seq.*
  advertising, 72
  Community legislation, 72
  Community trade, 70
  consumers, effect on, 70
  Court of Justice, 70, 71
  doorstep contracts, 73
  EEC, competence of, 69
  EEC Directive, 72
  free movement of goods, 70
  health and safety, 69, 70
  national rules, 70
  pharmaceutical products, 72, 73
  policy issues, 75
  political discretion, 72

151

Defamation Act 1952, 48
Defective products, 121, 132
Denmark
  product liability, 117
Department of Trade
  advertising, 62
Development risks, 134
Distortion
  competition of, 7
Doorstep contracts
  EEC Directive proposal, 73
  marketing practices, 73
Drinking water
  Directives on, 37
Drugs
  new, 133, 137
  product liability, 129–146
Duty-free imports, 34

EEC
  Consumer protection
    report of, 5
  EEC Directive (proposed)
    advertising
      class actions, 49
      remedies, 39, 47
      comparative advertising, 45
      trademark law, 46
  EEC Draft Directive
    product liability, 121–128
  EEC Treaty
    Article 2, 4, 26, 77
    Article 3, 78, 84
    Article 20, 83
    Article 30, 13, 32, 42, 43, 70, 71, 78, 89
    Article 34, 93
    Article 36, 13, 27, 42, 69, 85, 89
    Article 39, 31, 103
    Article 40, 103
    Article 59, 34, 89
    Article 61, 34
    Article 85, 32, 78, 103, 106
    Article 86, 32, 103, 106
    Article 87, 104, 105
    Article 90, 78
    Articles 92–94, 78
    Article 100, 1, 2, 3, 6, 8, 12, 15, 39, 70, 71, 78, 119
    Article 101, 8
    Article 113, 36
    Article 169, 13

EEC Treaty—*cont.*
  Article 173, 107
  Article 175, 107
  Article 177, 13, 105, 107
  Article 186, 107
  Article 189, 119
  Article 213, 21
  Article 235, 3, 4, 5, 6, 7, 12, 15, 16, 17, 71
  Consumer protection, 1, 13, 14, 25, 77
  free movement of goods, 77, 80–85
Energy consumption
  consumer information, 36
Environment and Consumer
  Protection Service, 27
Environmental protection, 15
Ethics committees, medical, 136
European Community Law Group
  advertising, report on, 53
European consumer law, 30, 98
European Consumer Law Group, 34
European Court of Justice
  advertising, unfair, 42
  Commission, relationship
    between, 106
  consumer protection, 13, 28
  jurisdiction, 106–107
European Economic Community.
  See EEC.
European Monetary System, 8
Eyssen Case, 88, 96

Foodstuffs
  additives, 88
  consumer information, 36
  harmonisation laws, 20, 21
  prices, 21
France
  product liability, 114, 118
Free movement of goods
  arbitrary discrimination, 86
  case law, 99–102
  Cassis de Dijon Case, 77
  commercial transactions, 90
  consumer interest, 79
  consumer law, 93
  consumer protection, 77
  discriminatory measures, 80
  distinctly applicable measures, 85
  EEC Treaty, 78
  exports, 93

Marketing practices—*cont.*
  premium offers, 71
  satellite television, 72
  tobacco advertising, 72
  unfair contract terms, 74
  uniformity, 83
Marketing surveillance
  pharmaceutical products, 140
Medical trials
  healthy volunteers, 137
Medicines Act 1968, 138
Messina Report, 3, 7
  social security charges, 3
Milk Marketing Board, 109
Monopolies and Mergers
  Commission, 107

National Consumer Council, 61
National Health Service, 130
National law
  Community law, relationship
    with, 104
Netherlands
  product liability, 115
Nisine Case, 28
"No fault" liability
  products, 122
Norway
  product liability, 117

Office of Fair Trading, 60, 61, 62, 107
  advertising survey, 63

Paris Convention 1883, 40
Passing-off, 49
Patents Act 1949, 130
Pearson Commission, 134, 142
Personal injury
  product liability, 129
Petrol
  Directives on, 37
Pharmaceutical products
  clinical trials, 137, 138
  compensation, 145–146
  consumer information, 35
  contracts, implied terms in, 130, 137
  ethics committees, 136
  generic prescribing, 141
  implied terms, 130–132
  industry standards, 133

Pharmaceutical products—*cont.*
  licence for, 138
  marketing practices, 72, 73, 140
  new, 136
  no-fault scheme, 141
  product liability, 129–146
    Germany, 115
    Sweden, 142
  product licence, 140
  public standards, 133
  research, 136
  state of the art, 132
  trials, medical, 137
  volunteer contract, 143
Premium offers
  marketing practices, 71
Prescriptions
  consumer rights, 130
  statutory obligations, 130
Price control
  free movement of goods, 90
Prices
  agricultural products, 31
  consumer goods, 31
  free competition, 32
  labelling, 33
  motor vehicles, 32
  pharmaceutical products, 32
  selective distribution, 32
Product liability, 113
  America, 135
  causation, 141
  clinical trials, 138
  commonwealth countries, 118
  compensation, 141
  contributory negligence, 127
  Convention, Council of Europe, 119, 120, 121–128
  damage to property, 120, 122
  death, 129, 134
  defences to, 126–128, 133
  development risks, 126, 134
  Draft Directive, 119, 120, 121–128
  ethics committees, 136
  European approach, 118
  highest standards, 134
  implied terms, 130–132, 137
  insurance, 123, 125
  law reform, 117, 121–128
  legislation, 113
    Austria, 116
    Belgium, 114

152

Product liability—*cont.*
  legislation—*cont.*
    common law countries, 116
    Denmark, 117
    France, 114
    German law countries, 115
    Germany, 115
    Ireland, 116
    Italy, 115
    Luxembourg, 114
    Netherlands, 115
    Norway, 117
    Roman law countries, 114
    Scandinavia, 117
    Sweden, 117
    Switzerland, 116
    United Kingdom, 116
  limitation of, 124
  limitation period, 128
  manufacturer, 123
  negligence action, 134, 137
  "no fault" liability, 122
  personal injuries, 120, 129
  pharmaceutical products,
    129–146
  policy, 121
  producer, liability of, 128
  product licence, 140
  safety, 127
  state of the art, 132
Product licence, 140
Product regulation
  consumer law, 97
Products
  new, 135
Public standards
  pharmaceutical products, 133

Research
  clinical trials, 138
  pharmaceutical products, 136
  Royal College of Physicians, 136

Safety
  product liability, 127
Sale of Goods Act 1979, 130
Sandoz Case, 28
Satellite advertising, 44
Self-regulation
  advertising
    bargain offers, 57
    criticisms of, 54

Self-regulation—*cont.*
  advertising—*cont.*
    legislation, 57
    motivation, 57
    positive aspects, 56
    definition, 54
State of the art
  product liability, 132
Strict liability
  pharmaceutical products, 133
Summit Conference 1972, 27
Supply of Goods and Services Act
  1982, 130
Surveys
  unfair advertising, 64
Sweden
  product liability, 117
Switzerland
  product liability, 116

Tax
  goods, on, 33
  Thalidomide Case, 117
Tobacco
  marketing practices, 72
Tort
  product liability, 132
Tourists
  policy on, 34
  protection of, 34
Trade Descriptions Act 1968,
  44
Trademarks
  comparative advertising, 46
Trademarks Act 1938, 47
Trade practices
  consumer law, 97
Trade union, 96

Unfair advertising, 39 *et seq.*
  consumer protection, 7
  damages for, 45
  definition of, 44, 45
  EEC Directive, proposed, 39
    et seq.
  marketing practices, 70
  self regulation policies, 53
  survey evidence, 64 *et seq.*
Unfair competition, 40, 90
  advertising, 50
  national regulations, 92
  policy, 50

153

Unfair contract terms
  Community proposals, 74
  consumer protection, 74
United Brands Case, 32
United Kingdom
  product liability, 116, 118

United States
  product liability, 135

Warnink Case, 49
Water
  Directives on, 37
World Medical Association, 136